W9-BAG-947

SPACE
SYSTEMS

The Big Bang Theory and Light Spectra

Rachel Keranen

Cavendish
Square
New York

Published in 2017 by Cavendish Square Publishing, LLC
243 5th Avenue, Suite 136, New York, NY 10016

Copyright © 2017 by Cavendish Square Publishing, LLC

First Edition

No part of this publication may be reproduced, stored in a retrieval system, or transmitted in any form or by any means—electronic, mechanical, photocopying, recording, or otherwise—without the prior permission of the copyright owner. Request for permission should be addressed to Permissions, Cavendish Square Publishing, 243 5th Avenue, Suite 136, New York, NY 10016. Tel (877) 980-4450; fax (877) 980-4454.

Website: cavendishsq.com

This publication represents the opinions and views of the author based on his or her personal experience, knowledge, and research. The information in this book serves as a general guide only. The author and publisher have used their best efforts in preparing this book and disclaim liability rising directly or indirectly from the use and application of this book.

CPSIA Compliance Information: Batch #CW17CSQ

All websites were available and accurate when this book was sent to press.

Library of Congress Cataloging-in-Publication Data
Names: Keranen, Rachel, author.
Title: The big bang theory and light spectra / Rachel Keranen.
Description: New York : Cavendish Square Publishing, [2017] |
Series: Space systems | Includes bibliographical references and index.
Identifiers: LCCN 2016034700 (print) | LCCN 2016040187 (ebook) |
ISBN 9781502622952 (library bound) | ISBN 9781502622969 (E-book)
Subjects: LCSH: Big bang theory--Juvenile literature. | Cosmology--Juvenile literature. | Cosmological distances--Juvenile literature. | Light--Wave-length--Juvenile literature. | Expanding universe--Juvenile literature.
Classification: LCC QB991.B54 K47 2017 (print) | LCC QB991.B54 (ebook) | DDC 523.1/8--dc23
LC record available at https://lccn.loc.gov/2016034700

Editorial Director: David McNamara
Editor: Caitlyn Miller
Copy Editor: Rebecca Rohan
Associate Art Director: Amy Greenan
Senior Designer: Alan Sliwinski
Production Coordinator: Karol Szymczuk
Photo Research: J8 Media

The photographs in this book are used by permission and through the courtesy of: Cover Sagittarius Production/Shutterstock.com; p. 4 NASA, ESA, HEIC, and The Hubble Heritage Team (STScI/AURA); pp. 10, 13 Print Collector/Hulton Archive/Getty Images; p. 15 Dorling Kindersley/Thinkstock.com; p. 17 Peter Hermes Furian/Shutterstock.com; p. 19 Herbert Hall Turner/File:Voyage in Space page272.jpg/Wikimedia Commons; p. 21 Phil Degginger/Alamy Stock Photo; p. 25 Mark Garlick/SPL/Getty Images; p. 28 Dana Berry/Skyworks Digital/NASA; p. 35 FT2/File:Massive star cutaway pre-collapse.png/Wikimedia Commons; p. 41 Jerry Cannon/NASA/File:Clouds of smoke around the 323rd Delta rocket on launch pad 17B.jpg/Wikimedia Commons; p. 43 NASA/JPL-Caltech/ESA/File:PIA16874-CobeWmapPlanckComparison-20130321.jpg/Wikimedia Commons; p. 48 Ferdinand Schmutzer/File:Albert Einstein 1921 by F Schmutzer.jpg/Wikimedia Commons; p. 63 Photos.com/Thinkstock.com; p. 64 F. W. Dyson, A. S. Eddington, and C. Davidson/File:1919 eclipse positive.jpg/Wikimedia Commons; p. 66 H. Armstrong Roberts/ClassicStock/Getty Images; p. 69 NASA/File:Horn Antenna-in Holmdel, New Jersey.jpeg/Wikimedia Commons; p. 70 NASA/File:Cobe vision2.jpg/Wikimedia Commons; p. 72 CERN; p. 75 Fermilab, Reidar Hahn/File:Fermilab.jpg/Wikimedia Commons; p. 76 Encyclopaedia Britannica/UIG/Getty Images; pp. 80, 93 Peter Ginter/Getty Images; p. 82 Lucas Taylor/CERN; p. 84 NASA/WMAP Science Team; p. 87 Henze, NASA/File:This visualization shows what Einstein envisioned.jpg/Wikimedia Commons; p. 99 Detlev van Ravenswaay/Science Source.

Printed in the United States of America

Contents

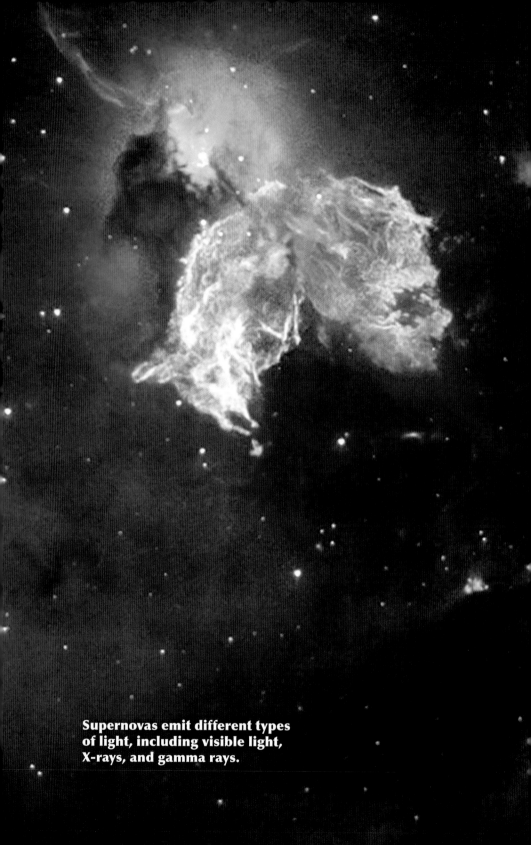

Supernovas emit different types
of light, including visible light,
X-rays, and gamma rays.

Introduction:
A Vast Expansion
of Time and Space

"The evolution of the world can be compared to a display of fireworks that has just ended: some few red wisps, ashes, and smoke. Standing on a cooled cinder, we see the slow fading of the suns, and we try to recall the vanished brilliance of the origin of the worlds."
— Georges Lemaître

I t is human nature to wonder where we come from and how the universe came to be. In the scientific world, that question has fallen largely to the physicists, astrophysicists, and astronomers who use the properties of light and space-time to study the universe in its earliest days.

The oldest stories of the universe, however, are mythologies based in superstition and supernatural events. Many of these myths describe gods as creative powers who shaped Earth and the universe. Over time this form of creation narrative began to change.

Ancient Greek scientists began to create more scientific theories in which they tried to describe the motion and elemental composition of the celestial bodies. The models were beautiful, but ultimately they did not match actual observation.

More than a millennium later, Nicolaus Copernicus began a scientific revolution with his assertion that Earth revolved around the sun. Over the next few hundred years, a new focus on observation-based hypotheses and advancements in optics and telescopes propelled the scientific world through discovery after discovery. It became possible to study not just the movement of the stars through the sky, but also the movement of stars and galaxies toward or away from Earth by studying their absorption of light. Our knowledge of light itself expanded as scientists discovered portions of the **electromagnetic spectrum** invisible to the naked eye, including longer wavelength **infrared** radiation and shorter wavelength **ultraviolet light**.

Still, many scientists, including the great physicist Albert Einstein, believed that the universe was infinite in size and time, with no beginning to speak of. For some scientists, to talk of a beginning suggested a return to the nonscientific creation mythologies.

Others worked through the equations in Einstein's general theory of relativity and said that the universe must be either contracting or expanding. Two such scientists, Alexander Friedmann and Georges Lemaître, both argued

that the universe was expanding and in the past had likely
been compressed in one very small, very dense region.
Lemaître suggested that the small, dense region was a
primeval atom that decayed into the matter that composes the
universe. Einstein dismissed both Friedmann and Lemaître
as scientists with accurate mathematics but terrible physics.

In 1929, American astronomer Edwin Hubble forever
changed the conversation with his discovery that the
galaxies in our universe are moving away from us at rate that
corresponds directly to their distance from us. The universe
is expanding, his observations showed, directly contradicting
the beliefs of Einstein and other physicists who preferred a
static model of the universe over time and space.

Friedmann had been largely ignored when he published
his data, and he died young, but Lemaître's theories got a
fresh breath of air after Hubble's analysis was published.
Einstein admitted his mistake and praised Lemaître's work,
and a new era of cosmology was born.

Physicist George Gamow, one of the only nuclear
physicists in America not pulled into the Manhattan Project
due to his Soviet roots, picked up the mantle and developed
what would become known as the big bang theory. Gamow
and his graduate student Ralph Alpher proposed a model
in which the early universe consisted of highly compressed
gas that expanded rapidly and gave birth to hydrogen and

helium, which fused into heavier elements and produced the universe we know today.

Curiously, it was Gamow's biggest scientific rival, Fred Hoyle, who named it the big bang theory. Hoyle preferred his own steady state theory, which suggested that the universe was infinitely old and homogenous (the same) throughout, and that new stars and galaxies formed in the gaps between galaxies that moved apart.

Over the course of the 1940s through the 1960s, however, the observational data stacked in favor of the big bang model. First, Arno Penzias and Robert Wilson detected a signal from the microwave portion of the electromagnetic spectrum spread evenly across the entire sky and eventually realized the radiation was the echo of the big bang. Analysis of unique **radio galaxies**, which primarily emit radiation in the radio portion of the electromagnetic spectrum, showed that the universe was not homogenous as Hoyle and his colleagues had proposed. Hoyle himself contributed to the big bang model by developing the theory of stellar **nucleosynthesis.** This theory describes how stars produce heavy elements and, when they die, scatter those elements throughout the cosmos.

The data also helped flesh out how elements heavier than helium formed and how galaxies formed from the earliest conditions of the universe.

Today, though we can't see directly back to the time the universe was created, scientists have a good sense of how the universe evolved back to 10^{-38} seconds after the big bang. Scientists have also improved their understanding of the big bang as a moment that came before a rapid inflation of time and space. This cosmic inflation took the universe from a millimeter to astronomical in scale in a fraction of a second.

In those early moments, the extreme heat and energy kept all matter in the most elementary states. As the universe cooled over the next several hundred thousand years, those particles formed into atoms and eventually into clumps of matter. Those clumps became large-scale structures, like galaxies and stars. Over thirteen billion years these structures have developed into the universe we know today.

As much as we have developed the model, questions remain. What powered that cosmic inflation? Can we prove that it happened? As we understand them, classical physics and quantum physics break down in the extreme conditions of the big bang. What are the laws of physics at that moment, and are there laws that unite classical physics and quantum physics in the theory of everything that Einstein was trying to find when he died? What came before the big bang, and how can we study it? What came before that?

It's exciting work for physicists who are studying radiation from the big bang for details of the early universe and those who use particle accelerators to recreate the conditions of the big bang. Research is constantly underway, and the model of the big bang is continually being expanded and revised.

In Japan's earliest written record, the brother-and-sister gods Izanagi and Izanami are said to have created the Japanese archipelago.

Early Predictions

O ur ability to think about our existence is part of what makes us human. Throughout the history of our species, different cultures have developed different explanations of how the universe came to be.

As science and technology advanced through the 1800s and 1900s, physicists and astronomers paired this curiosity with the advancements in light spectra, telescopes, and nuclear physics to create a scientific explanation for the structure and evolution of the universe.

MYTHOLOGIES AND COSMOLOGIES

The earliest explanations of how the universe came to be the way it is today were driven by superstition and divine intervention. Over time, this gave way to increasingly more scientific attempts at describing the universe, leading up to the Scientific Revolution that forever changed the way we study and understand the universe.

Creation Mythologies

According to the *Kojiki*, Japan's earliest written record, the universe began as shapeless chaos, out of which arose particles of light and matter. The particles of light rose to form the top of the universe, other particles formed the clouds and heavens, and the heaviest particles formed Earth. Numerous gods emerged from the heavens, and two of these gods created the Japanese archipelago.

In Christian scripture, God creates Earth and the heavens in six days. The first man and woman, Adam and Eve, fall from his favor and are banished from the idyllic garden of Eden. Adam and Eve go on to have children and begin human history.

Creation stories vary by culture and there are many different versions from different times and places, tied together by the presence of divine and supernatural elements. There are no testable hypotheses, and thus the mythologies exist outside of the scientific method.

Ancient Greek Astronomy

The ancient Greeks were some of the first to move from mythology to a more scientific approach. Yet the Greeks were not always accurate.

Ptolemy believed that the planets were nested in revolving solid spheres.

The Greek philosopher Aristotle (384 BCE to 322 BCE) proposed an understanding of the universe that was influential in Western Europe for over a thousand years. Aristotle said that the universe consisted of fifty-five concentric (nesting) spheres, from Earth at the center to spheres for each planet and one for the fixed stars to the outermost sphere of a so-called Prime Mover (a divine creator). The motion of the Prime Mover created a constant velocity that moved all of the interior spheres, which revolved around Earth.

Aristotle's method didn't account for irregularities in the movement of planets and stars. Yet it did make sense at a high level. From the observer's perspective, Earth seems to remain still while the sun and other celestial objects move around it.

The Greek scientist and mathematician Claudius Ptolemy (100 CE to 168 CE) tried to account for the irregularities by modifying Aristotle's concentric spheres model. He included a second, smaller orbit, called the epicycle, that each planet moves around as it completes its larger orbit around Earth. Using the notion of epicycles and other modifications, Ptolemy could account for apparent reversals in planetary motion. Today we now know these reversals are due to the different speeds of Earth and other bodies that orbit the sun.

The Scientific Revolution

In 1543, Polish mathematician and astronomer Nicolaus Copernicus published *De revolutionibus orbium coelestium*. The book presented a heliocentric (sun-centered) model of the universe and launched a scientific revolution. The Scientific Revolution focused on observation and testable hypotheses; it continued from the 1500s to the 1700s.

Copernicus's work was followed by big contributions from Johannes Kepler, Isaac Newton, and others who helped flesh out laws of physics, optics, and astronomy (such as the first law of gravity and the elliptical orbits of planets around the sun). The new knowledge and methods that came out of the Scientific Revolution improved scientists' understanding of both light and the cosmos. It also provided a foundation for the discoveries that followed throughout the centuries.

LIGHT SPECTRA

While scientists such as Kepler studied celestial motion and advanced astronomy and physics, other scientists studied the properties of light. Understanding light was a key part of studying the beginning of the universe.

Two important discoveries about light were made in the seventeenth century. Scientists realized that light is made up

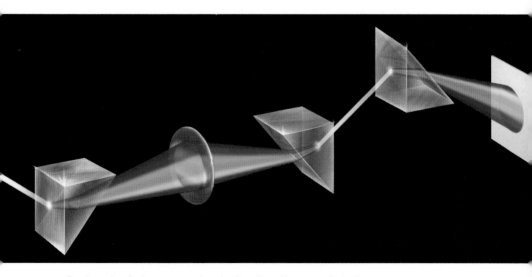

To show that light contained multiple colors, Newton split light into a spectrum and then combined it back into white light.

of separate wavelengths and that light travels at a finite speed. They also realized that different elements produce different colors of light when burned.

Before the 1670s, many scientists believed that the reason white light passing through a prism creates a rainbow was because the prism itself colored the light. In 1672, Isaac Newton published the results of experiments he conducted showing that white light is made up of separate colors and the prism refracts each color differently. Today we know that those colors correspond to a wavelength of light.

Up until the 1670s, it was also commonly believed that light moved infinitely fast and appeared without delay. In 1676, Danish astronomer Ole Rømer set up an experiment designed to measure the speed of light and prove that light moves at a finite speed.

First, Rømer studied the eclipse of Jupiter's moon Io and noticed that Io was often either early or late to appear from behind Jupiter. The time between eclipses became shorter (that is, Io appeared earlier than predicted) as Earth moved closer to Jupiter. The interval became longer as Earth moved farther from Jupiter. This indicated that the difference in Io's appearance was due to the varying distance its light had to travel between Jupiter and Earth. Therefore, light must move at a finite speed.

Rømer estimated that light moves at 132,973 miles per second (214,000 kilometers per second). Today, the speed of light is measured at 186,000 miles per second (299,792.458 kilometers per second).

The Full Spectrum

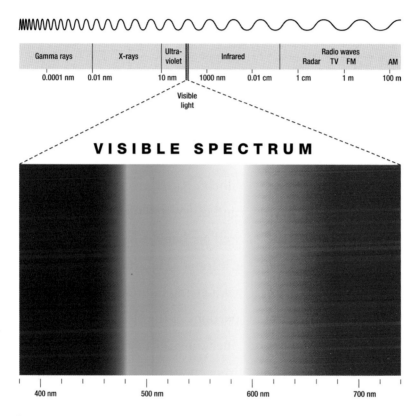

Radiation from any portion of the electromagnetic spectrum travels at the speed of light but at different frequencies and wavelengths.

Before 1800, the kind of light that scientists studied belonged to the visible portion of the electromagnetic spectrum. Visible light is only a fraction of the light (or radiation) that exists, however.

In 1800, the astronomer Sir William Herschel discovered there was light beyond the visible spectrum when he began an experiment designed to measure the heat of different colors of light. He used a glass prism to separate sunlight into its separate colors and placed a thermometer under each color. He placed another thermometer next to the red light where no visible light appeared. The red light was the hottest color of visible light, but the thermometer beyond it measured even hotter. Herschel had discovered the infrared portion of the spectrum.

A year later, Johann Wilhelm Ritter investigated the other end of the spectrum and discovered ultraviolet light. In 1867, James Clerk Maxwell predicted a light with a longer wavelength than the infrared. Heinrich Hertz proved Maxwell correct by producing radio waves in 1887. Over time, the remaining portions of the electromagnetic spectrum were discovered, including microwaves, X-rays, and gamma rays. The electromagnetic spectrum is typically arranged based on wavelength and frequency of radiation. It is arranged from the low frequency, long wavelength radio waves to the high frequency, short wavelength gamma ray radiation.

The simplest type of light-emitting object is called a **blackbody**. A blackbody is a theoretical object that absorbs and emits all wavelengths of light, producing a continuous spectrum. As the temperature of a blackbody goes up, the

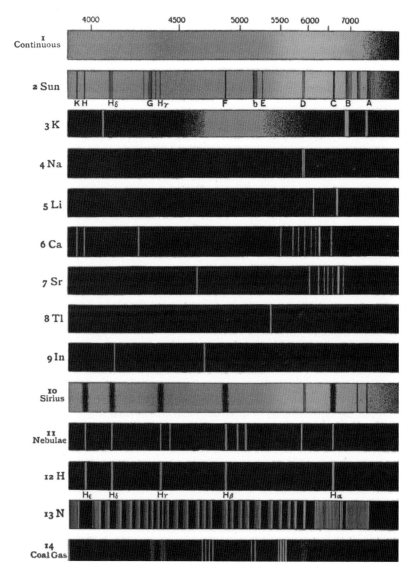

The sun's spectrum is not of radiation directly from its surface but of radiation that has passed through the sun's atmosphere.

amount of energy it emits increases and the peak wavelength (the wavelength where the most radiation is emitted) decreases. No perfect blackbodies exist, but a common example of an object that behaves like a blackbody is an electric stove. As the burner heats up, the coil transforms from black to a glowing red.

In reality, not all spectra are continuous. Objects produce different types of spectra based on their temperature and composition. A nineteenth-century German physicist named Gustav Kirchhoff created three laws of spectroscopy, which state that:

- A hot solid, liquid, or gas under high pressure produces a continuous spectrum (with light of all wavelengths).
- A low-density, hot gas produces an emission line spectrum.
- A continuous spectrum viewed behind a low-density, cool gas creates an absorption line spectrum.

Kirchhoff did not know that atoms have separate energy levels, but later developments in physics explained the phenomena Kirchhoff's spectroscopy laws describe. When a beam of light passes through an atom in a low-energy state, the atom will absorb a **photon** (particle of light) with the

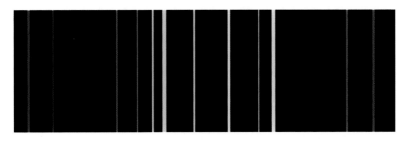

An emission spectrum shows the precise wavelengths of light given off by a hot gas when those wavelengths are studied using a prism.

exact amount of energy required for the atom's electron to jump from its current state to the next highest energy level. That photon disappears from the light beam, creating a dark line (or absorption line) in the light beam's spectrum.

Similarly, when the same atom is in an "excited" or higher energy state, that atom's electron will eventually fall back to the lowest-energy ground state. In doing so, it releases photons with the same amount of energy as it previously absorbed to attain that higher energy state. This produces an emission spectrum with lines of emitted light in the exact places where light is absorbed in an absorption spectrum.

Each element has unique absorption and emission lines in their light spectra. Between 1855 and 1863, Kirchhoff and fellow physicist Robert Bunsen conducted the first investigation of flame spectra using a gas Bunsen burner and a **spectroscope**, an instrument that can produce spectra of light. They analyzed thousands of spectral lines and, in doing so, discovered new elements including rubidium and cesium.

Using his knowledge of element-specific spectral lines, Kirchhoff analyzed sunlight and found that the sun contained familiar elements including sodium, magnesium, iron, and calcium. In 1869, Joseph Norman Lockyer studied solar spectra and discovered that the sun emitted helium, an element not found on Earth until 1895.

In the 1860s, the husband-and-wife team William and Margaret Huggins used spectroscopy to show that the elements in the stars were elements found on Earth. The Hugginses also showed that spectroscopy could be used to measure star velocity by combining the analysis of light spectra with the Doppler effect. The Doppler effect was discovered in 1842, and it's the reason sound of an ambulance changes as it moves toward and away from an observer. When an object is moving toward an observer, the wavelengths of sound it emits are shorter. When the object moves away from an observer, the sound is emitted from an increasingly distant point and the wavelengths are thus longer.

A similar effect is observed in wavelengths of light. When an object is moving toward an observer, the space between the object and the observer is compressed, and the wavelengths are shortened. The light thus appears **blueshifted**, or shifted to the "bluer" end of the electromagnetic spectrum. When an object is moving away from an observer (the more common scenario), the space and wavelengths are expanded and the light therefore

The Double-Slit Experiment

Is light a particle or a wave? The double-slit experiment, first performed in the 1920s, shows that light and matter can display behaviors of both particles and waves.

In the double-slit experiment, a beam of light is fired toward a barrier that has two parallel slits cut into it. Behind the barrier is a detector screen. If light behaved like particles do, the expected result would be two parallel lines on the detector screen directly behind the two slits in the barrier. However, the actual result of the experiment shows *bands* of light across the screen.

The result shows that light (and matter, when the experiment is conducted with a stream of electrons) has properties of waves, which can split and combine. When photons pass through the slits, their wave nature creates ripples, just as a speedboat creates ripples as it passes through a lake. These ripples cross over one another, cancel each other out in some places, amplify each other in some places, and create a band pattern on the detector screen.

And yet, like a particle, the photons pass through one slit or the other and hit the screen in separate places. Having some properties of waves and some properties of particles is called the **wave-particle duality**.

appears **redshifted**, or shifted to the "redder" end of the electromagnetic spectrum. Scientists can measure whether an object is moving toward or away from Earth and how fast it is moving by comparing the known absorption spectrum of an object's chemical composition with the observed absorption spectrum of an object in space.

The Hugginses could see that the star Sirius had nearly identical absorption lines as the sun but were just 0.015 percent greater in wavelength. Sirius was not made of different elements, they hypothesized. They said it was just moving away from Earth and so it appeared to have slightly longer wavelengths of light. Using this technique, it was now possible to measure the velocity of any star (and galaxy) as it moved toward or away from Earth.

FOUNDATIONAL PHYSICS

The ability to study the universe using properties of light set the stage for the big bang theory. The first versions of the theory appeared in papers published independently by Alexander Friedmann and Georges Lemaître in the 1920s. The timing is no coincidence: both were inspired by the work of Albert Einstein and his 1915 theory of general relativity.

The Roots of the Big Bang Theory

According to Einstein's theory of general relativity, gravity was not a matter of objects attracting one another, as Isaac

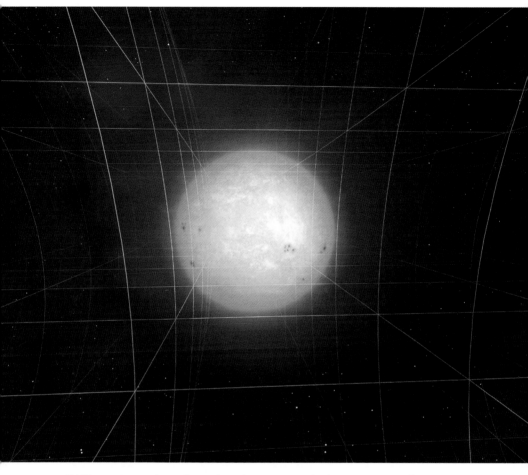

NASA experiments have shown that when a massive body rotates, gravity's distortion effects cause space and time to swirl around it.

Newton had said in 1687. Einstein believed gravity was the effect of mass on something called space-time. Mass curves space-time much like a bowling ball curves a trampoline surface, and objects move in straight lines through space-time. When space-time curves, an object's straight path follows the curve of space-time.

Einstein's theory of general relativity also provided a framework for understanding the universe as a whole. Some solutions to his equations showed that the universe was expanding, while others showed that it was contracting. Einstein believe the universe was not expanding or contracting, so he added a **cosmological constant** to balance his equations.

In 1922, Russian mathematician and meteorologist Alexander Friedmann used Einstein's equations to hypothesize an expanding universe that began with an initial expansion. However, Friedmann had no evidence. He was a mathematician instead of an astronomer, and he contracted typhoid and died in 1925. As a result, his work was mostly ignored.

A few years later, a young Belgian mathematician (and Catholic priest) named Georges Lemaître began working on the general theory of relativity while studying at Cambridge University in the 1920s. As Friedmann had found, Lemaître's calculations showed that the universe had to be either shrinking or expanding. Lemaître looked at other astronomical clues for supporting evidence. Objects outside of our galaxy were redshifted, which meant that they were moving away from Earth. Lemaître concluded that the universe was expanding and, if objects were moving away from one another, they had once been much closer to one another.

In 1927, Lemaître proposed what he called the "Primeval Atom Hypothesis," which stated that the universe began as a single dense primeval atom that exploded into radioactive fragments. The fragments radioactively decayed to form the atoms that we know today and expanded over time. That expansion was responsible for the observed redshift, Lemaître wrote. Objects were not moving through space; space was expanding, and the distance between objects was growing greater.

Lemaître published his paper in a little-known Belgian journal and few read it. Lemaître sent his work to Einstein, who told him his mathematics were correct but his physics were terrible. Years later, Lemaître's work received greater attention when Arthur Eddington, his former professor at Cambridge, published a favorable commentary on Lemaître's work in 1930. Eddington followed up with a shortened English translation in 1931.

When Friedmann and Lemaître proposed an expanding universe, they were both laughed at. In time, however, new discoveries in astronomy and physics support their ideas.

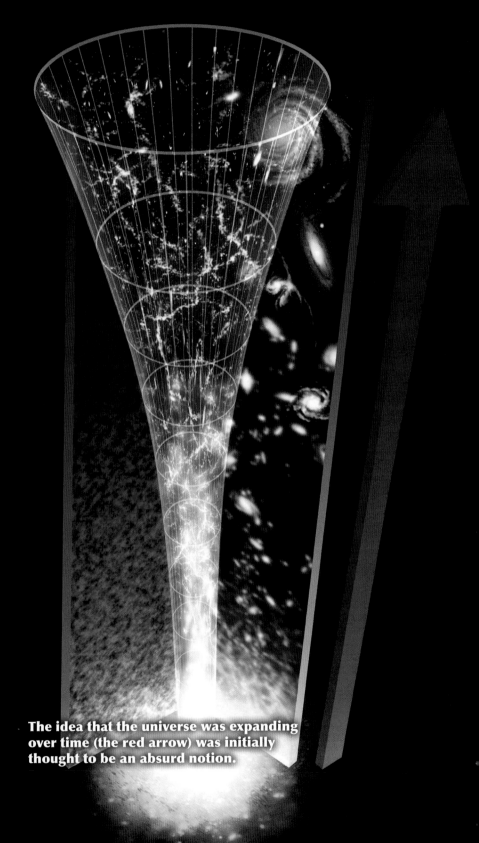

The idea that the universe was expanding over time (the red arrow) was initially thought to be an absurd notion.

The Modern Understanding of the Big Bang Theory

F riedmann and Lemaître formed the first theories of an expanding universe in the 1920s. At the time, their theories seemed radical. Just a decade later, those theories began to seem more and more like obvious conclusions based on new data.

THE BIG BANG THEORY

The universe, early big bang theorists said, began as a very small, dense point. It expanded rapidly, eventually forming structures such as the galaxies, stars, and planetary systems we observe today. In the early days of the big bang theory, this is essentially all its supporters proposed. There was little understanding of how this process happened. (Note that the theory wasn't actually called the big bang theory until 1949.)

As technology advanced in the twentieth century, with bigger telescopes, better photography, and instruments that could measure electromagnetic radiation beyond the visible spectrum, more and more data came in that supported the big bang theory. It all started with American astronomer Edwin Hubble's analysis of galaxies and the speeds at which they were moving away (called their recession speeds) from our vantage point on Earth.

Hubble's Great Discovery

In the late 1920s, Hubble sat at the eyepiece of the telescope at the Mount Wilson Observatory in Pasadena, California. The observatory had the largest telescope in the world at the time, the Hooker Telescope. Through it, Hubble had already made one major observation when he discovered that the universe consisted of galaxies beyond the Milky Way. In 1929, Hubble and his assistant Milton Humason published another shocking paper. Those other galaxies were moving away from Earth, and the farther away a galaxy was from Earth, the faster it was moving.

To reach this conclusion, Hubble first determined the distance to dozens of galaxies. He used a practice common at the time that relied on finding Cepheid variable stars (a type of pulsating star) in each galaxy. Astronomer Henrietta Leavitt Swan had previously found a relationship between how often a Cepheid variable star pulses and its **intrinsic**

luminosity, or absolute brightness. By comparing the intrinsic luminosity of a Cepheid variable star to its apparent (observed) luminosity, an astronomer can estimate distance just as we estimate the distance to an oncoming car at night based on how bright its headlights appear.

For more distant galaxies, which were too far off to observe Cepheid variable stars, Hubble identified the brightest star and used its apparent brightness to roughly estimate the distance to the galaxy.

Once he had calculated the distance to each galaxy, he plotted the distance against their **radial velocities** (the speed the galaxy was moving along the line of sight of an observer), determined by studying the redshift of each galaxy. The data was clear: galaxies were moving away from us at a speed that directly correlated to their distance. The farther the galaxy was from us now, the faster away it was moving.

Hubble himself was not interested thinking about the consequences of his results, but this much was clear: the universe was expanding. Taking the rate of expansion Hubble found (called the **Hubble Constant**), the universe was calculated to be 1.8 billion years old. In other words, it had a beginning.

After Hubble's data was made public, those who believed the universe had been expanding over time finally had scientific evidence supporting their theory. That evidence was strong enough to convince many that the big bang model of the universe was correct, including Albert Einstein. In 1931, Einstein visited Mount Wilson as Hubble's guest and endorsed the big bang expansion model of the universe. He dismissed his cosmological constant, calling it the biggest blunder of his life. He also came out in support of Lemaître, who suddenly was famous after years without recognition.

Still, the big bang model of the universe was not widely accepted. Hubble's data was the only evidence, and it predicted a universe that was just 1.8 billion years old. The Earth had rocks over a billion years older than that. How could a universe be younger than its parts? Over the next several decades, scientists would investigate the conditions of the early universe and search for evidence that supported the big bang theory of expansion—or its opposing model, the steady state theory.

Gamow and Alpher

The Ukraine-born American physicist George Gamow began his big bang research in the 1940s. Gamow didn't accept Lemaître's theory of a super atom breaking down into smaller parts. Gamow had worked with other scientists studying **nuclear fusion** and **nuclear fission** (the formation and breakdown of atomic nuclei, respectively). The research, including that conducted independently by Carl von Weizsäcker and Hans Bethe, helped reveal an explanation of element formation in the big bang model.

In nuclear fusion, lighter nuclei combine to form a heavier nucleus. The combination causes a release of energy. When Gamow began investigating how elements form, it had already been shown that hydrogen nuclei fuse to form helium inside of stars. Yet fusion in stars alone couldn't be the reason for all of the helium in the universe. Also, no one understood how elements heavier than helium formed.

Gamow thought perhaps the very early universe could explain the abundance of helium and the formation of other elements. When Gamow imagined the timeline of the universe in reverse, he saw that the universe would grow increasingly dense as it contracted. Heat would be generated, creating the hot, dense conditions required for nuclear fusion. Because of the heat of the early universe, Gamow predicted, matter started as a very hot, dense gas made of neutrons. As the universe expanded, the neutrons would decay into protons, electrons, and **neutrinos**. As the universe rapidly cooled, Gamow hypothesized that a process called nucleosynthesis occurred.

Gamow, while working at George Washington University, teamed up with Ralph Alpher, a physics graduate student, to calculate the rapidly changing conditions of the early, expanding universe. Alpher's calculations showed that at the end of the nucleosynthesis phase of the big bang, there would be one helium nucleus for every ten hydrogen nuclei. Alpher's prediction corresponded with the observed ratio of helium to hydrogen, and it provided an additional bit of support for the big bang model.

Gamow and Alpher published their work on April 1, 1948. Two major problems remained in the model, however. First, Gamow and Alpher had theorized that the expanding, cooling universe could create heavier and heavier elements, but they were unable to show that any element heavier than helium could be created through this process. Hydrogen and helium make up 99 percent of the ordinary matter in the universe, but there are many heavier elements as well, such as iron, gold, and silver, which we encounter in our daily lives. How did they come to be? Second, the age of the universe at this point was still calculated to be 1.8 billion years, which was much too young.

SUPPORTING EVIDENCE

Over the four decades after Gamow and Alpher published their paper in 1948, scientists made a series of discoveries that added further support to the big bang theory.

The Birth of Heavier Elements

One of the big bang theory's biggest opponents figured out a solution to the problem of how heavy elements are created. The big bang itself was only responsible for producing hydrogen, helium, lithium, and trace amounts of beryllium. It was known that stars also fuse hydrogen to create helium.

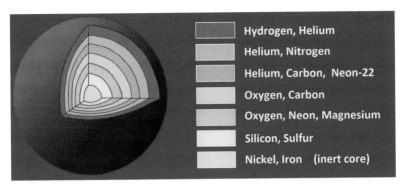

	Hydrogen, Helium
	Helium, Nitrogen
	Helium, Carbon, Neon-22
	Oxygen, Carbon
	Oxygen, Neon, Magnesium
	Silicon, Sulfur
	Nickel, Iron (inert core)

As new elements form within a star, they create layers called "shells."

As stars go through their lifecycle, they periodically run out of fuel at their core, contract, and heat up again due to that contraction. As a result, Cambridge physicist Fred Hoyle predicted, stars could be the responsible for the creation of heavy elements as well.

When a star runs out of its supply of hydrogen (meaning all available hydrogen has been converted to helium), its temperature would rise until it could burn that helium, which eventually converts into carbon and oxygen. As the star gets hotter and hotter over its lifespan, heavier and heavier elements form, all the way up to iron. (We know today that elements heavier than iron are formed from reactions in the supernova explosions of the most massive stars.) When a star dies, it sends that mixture of elements into the cosmos. This mixture is the material from which new stars form.

Hoyle's calculations accounted for the observed amounts of different elements. The lightweight hydrogen and helium are the first to form and are the most abundant elements while medium-weight oxygen and iron are relatively common and the heavier gold, silver, and platinum are relatively rare.

To support his theory, Hoyle had to prove that helium could fuse into carbon, something no scientist had previously been able to show. (This difficulty had been a roadblock for Gamow and Alpher in advancing their theory of nucleosynthesis after the big bang.) The key relied on finding an excited state of the most common carbon isotope, carbon-12. (Isotopes are variants of an element with different numbers of neutrons. For example, carbon-12 has six protons and six neutrons while carbon-13 has six protons and seven neutrons.)

In 1954, Hoyle predicted that an excited state of carbon-12 could form from the known isotopes helium-4 and beryllium-8. This excited form of carbon-12 would have to have a very specific state, specifically 7.65 MeV (mega **electron volts**, a unit of energy), for Hoyle's theory to work.

Hoyle asked American physicist Willy Fowler to help him prove the state existed. Fowler showed that it did, solving yet another cosmological mystery.

While Hoyle's work lent support to the big bang theory, Hoyle himself was one of the leaders of the opposing side, the steady state theory. Hoyle proposed the steady state theory in 1948—with fellow British scientists Sir Hermann Bondi and Thomas Gold—and worked on it for years afterward.

Steady state theorists argued that the universe is constantly expanding (as Hubble had shown) but maintains the same density and structure at all times and in all places. New matter is continuously created to form new stars and galaxies, so while galaxies might be moving farther away, new galaxies are popping up in the gaps to create an overall consistent character to the universe.

This theory faced challenges, however, including the position of radio galaxies. Radio galaxies, which primarily emit radiation in the radio frequency range of the electromagnetic spectrum, were thought to have formed before other types of galaxies. If the steady state theory was true, these unique galaxies should be evenly distributed throughout the universe. If the big bang theory was true, these galaxies should be found only on the far edges of the universe, where light from billions of years ago is just beginning to reach us. In 1961, astronomer Martin Ryle found that most radio galaxies are at the far edges of the universe and formed in the early universe, supporting the big bang theory over the steady state theory.

An Aging Universe

A major obstacle remained: The calculated age of the universe was younger than some of the rocks on Earth. New research, however, showed that the universe was much older than Hubble's data suggested.

First, the physicist Walter Baade performed a new analysis of galaxy recession. The Hooker Telescope, while bigger than any in its day, was not big enough to reveal that there were two types of Cepheid variable stars, one consistently brighter than the other. Hubble had performed his calculations using the brighter stars, assuming they were dimmer than they were. As a result, his calculations showed that galaxies were much closer than they really are (as would be required for a "dim" star to appear so bright). Using the refined understanding of Cepheid variable stars, Baade revised the age of the universe to be at least 3.6 billion years old.

Baade's student Allan Sandage further refined that estimate using a more accurate method of finding the brightest stars in the most distant galaxies. In the 1950s, Sandage found the universe was at least 5.5 billion years old. Over the next few decades, as he made more and more measurements of the size of the universe and its expansion rate, he revised his estimate of the universe's age to between 10 billion and 20 billion years old. Now the universe wasn't just older than Earth, it was old enough to realistically contain all the stars and galaxies as well.

The Echo of the Big Bang

The most exciting and convincing supporting evidence for the big bang theory came from two scientists at Bell Labs in

New Jersey. Bell Labs, the research and development wing of AT&T, was formed in the 1920s and combined commercial research with pure science research.

In 1963, Arno Penzias and Robert Wilson began working with a new radio telescope called the Horn Antenna. They expected to detect a faint glow from the Milky Way and absolutely nothing from empty space, which they assumed would be as cold as absolute zero (–273.15 degrees Celsius, –459.67 degrees Fahrenheit, or 0 degrees kelvin). Instead, no matter where they aimed their antenna, they detected a mysterious signal.

Penzias and Wilson wanted to remove the noise so that they could get the most precise measurements possible. They spent a year troubleshooting, including checking and rewiring every piece of equipment over again and sweeping pigeon droppings from two roosting pigeons. They went as far as mailing the pigeons out of the area, but because the pigeons were homing pigeons, they flew right back.

Penzias told a scientist at the Massachusetts Institute of Technology about the strange noise, and soon the scientist called him back. A team at Princeton had predicted that the radiation left over from the big bang would measure about 3 K (actually 2.728 K), the measurement Penzias and Wilson were detecting from every direction. Ralph Alpher and his colleague Robert Herman had also predicted the **cosmic microwave background** in 1948. They found that the leftover light should have stretched from approximately $\frac{1}{1000}$ of a millimeter at 300,000 years post-big bang to 1 millimeter today. It would, at this wavelength, appear in the microwave portion of the electromagnetic spectrum. It wasn't hard to find with the equipment of the 1960s, but nobody had been looking for it. Most people, when they detected the faint noise, just chalked it up as "noise" and left it at that. This energy is called the cosmic microwave background radiation, or the CMB.

The discovery was an enormous boost for the big bang theory, and Penzias and Wilson later won a Nobel Prize in Physics for their work.

The Seeds of Modern Galaxies

The final major question was the origin of galaxies. There was evidence of leftover heat from the big bang, as seen in the measurements of the CMB. There was evidence in favor of a continuously expanding universe that was billions of years old. There was also evidence of stars' creation of heavy elements. Nothing, however, yet showed how galaxies could form after the big expansion of time and space and create the stars where stellar nucleosynthesis took place.

The signal that Penzias and Wilson detected had been a steady signal no matter which direction they looked. Big bang theory supporters hoped that with a better instrument, they could find variations in the microwave radiation. The

COBE could take measurements one hundred times more accurate than detectors launched on balloons.

variations in the radiation would show that there were hotter and colder regions of the early universe, which were correlated to the gravitational field of the early universe. (Gravity affects density, which affects temperature.) Higher gravity regions of space would attract more matter and eventually collapse to form structures.

A cosmologist at the University of California at Berkeley, George Smoot, was one of the scientists hoping to find such variations. The trouble was that Earth's atmosphere interfered with the measurements. Smoot tried many ways to get above the atmosphere to gather data. In 1976, he attached a differential microwave radiometer (which will be discussed further in the next chapter) to high-flying U2 spy planes. The planes could not fly long enough to collect the amount of data Smoot needed, however. (He did find that the Milky Way is moving at a speed of more than one million miles per hour relative to the universe, however, so it was not a scientific loss!) Smoot would have to go into space to get the data he needed.

The initial NASA launch of Smoot's instrument was scheduled for 1988, but it was delayed after the Challenger shuttle exploded in 1986. Smoot's team considered sending their equipment up in a French rocket, but NASA didn't want to let an American science project go up in a French rocket. In December 1989, Smoot was finally able to send his instrument, the Cosmic Background Explorer (COBE) satellite into space on a small NASA rocket. COBE orbited

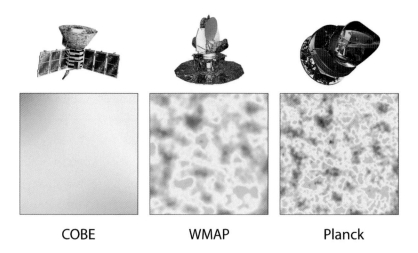

COBE   WMAP   Planck

The CMB measurements were progressively refined by results from the WMAP and Planck missions in 2001 and 2009, respectively.

the Earth at an altitude of about 560 miles (901 km), where it gathered data through 1990 and 1991. In December 1991, after two years in space, COBE completed its first full sky map.

The data showed small ripples in the temperature of the CMB. It was exactly the result that big bang supporters needed.

Smoot announced the results on April 23, 1992, at the American Physical Society in Washington, DC. In the autobiography he wrote for the Nobel Prize literature (which he won for detecting the CMB fluctuations), Smoot wrote: "The detected ripples in space-time, which measure about a part in 100,000 or 30 millionths of a degree differences in temperature, started as small lumps (quantum

Photographing the
Embryo Universe

When George Smoot and his team analyzed the data sent back by the COBE satellite, he took special care to make sure that the analysis was as thorough as possible. Edwin Hubble's analysis of galaxy distances, for example, was modified repeatedly in later years. Hubble disliked the revisions to his work. The modifications only further supported the big bang model as they extended the age of the universe, but Hubble was embarrassed to have committed errors in his work. Smoot knew that the data his team gathered would be important—either the CMB had fluctuations that could lead to galaxy formation or the CMB was not actually the relic of the big bang that people thought it was. He wanted to get it right.

To encourage others to seek errors and speak up, Smoot offered two free plane tickets to any place in the world for anyone who found an error in the data. The team also worked in secrecy until Smoot was sure that the CMB was showing cosmic fluctuations instead of signals from something like the sun or the instruments themselves.

The work was very challenging and required enormous precision. Smoot described searching for fluctuations in the CMB as "listening for a whisper during a noisy beach party while radios blare, waves crash, people yell, dogs bark, and dune buggies roar."

Smoot was able to remove outside signals, and he found that the signal of the CMB fit the predicted fluctuations. There are about 100 billion galaxies in the universe and about 100 billion stars in our own galaxy, and it all came from tiny quantum fluctuations in the earliest stages of the universe that expanded over time.

fluctuations) but over time expanded to the immense size that COBE observed."

PUTTING IT TOGETHER

Today, with the work done by Gamow, Alpher, Hoyle, Penzias, Wilson, Smoot, and many more, we have a much more complete model of the big bang.

According to the theory, about 13.77 billion years ago the universe began with a rapid inflation of an extremely small and extremely dense region. While the cosmological model is called the big bang model, it is best thought of as a sudden appearance of space and time rather than as a bang or an explosion.

In the first 10^{-34} seconds, the universe expanded into a universe stretching beyond the view of our largest telescopes. During the period of inflation, quantum mechanical fluctuations (the laws of **quantum mechanics** describe the behavior of particles) gave rise to the density fluctuations that later formed the large-scale structures in our universe, such as galaxies.

At first, all matter was in its most elementary state with pairs of particles and **antiparticles** appearing and destroying each other. (All particles are believed to have an antiparticle that is identical except for possessing an opposite charge.) It is thought that for every billion antiparticles, there are a billion and one particles and thus after destruction, matter still remained. As the universe cooled from its initial state, the cooler temperatures began to prevent particle and antiparticle pairs from appearing. Eventually the universe was just the matter leftover.

Big bang nucleosynthesis took place over the first ten minutes of the universe's lifetime as free protons and neutrons began to form light elements. Hydrogen comprised 75 percent of the matter formed. The remainder consisted of helium and lithium and trace amounts of beryllium.

For the first 380,000 years, the universe was too hot for the electrons to attach to the light nuclei to create atoms. The universe therefore consisted of a dark and opaque plasma, as the radiation (light) passing through the universe was scattered by the free electrons and could not escape. Once the universe had cooled to about 3000 K, the electrons and nuclei combined to form neutral atoms (a process called **recombination**) and light finally could travel freely and become visible (a process called **decoupling**). The light released in this period is visible today as the cosmic microwave background (CMB).

For a time, the universe was transparent but there were no stars shining, a period known as the cosmic dark ages. After the period of decoupling, the atoms gathered into molecules. The regions of greater density, which correlated to cooler temperatures, attracted more matter (including the poorly understood **dark matter** that dominates the universe). These regions grew in size and eventually became dense clouds of gas and dust separated by voids. After a few hundred million years, as the gravity of the dense regions became stronger than the force of the regions' internal gas pressure, the clouds of gas and dust collapsed and formed the first galaxies and stars.

The first generation of stars are thought to have been between thirty to three hundred times as massive as the sun with lifespans of just a few million years. These massive stars formed the first heavy elements through stellar nucleosynthesis, and when they died, they exploded as supernovas. Those supernovas sent heavy elements into the cosmos, providing material for subsequent stars and planetary systems to form. This created a more heterogeneous (diverse) composition of the universe.

Today, the big bang model is widely accepted among scientists as the best cosmological explanation of our universe. There is significant evidence that supports the big bang theory, made possible by numerous scientists over the twentieth century and advancing technology. New technology provided deeper and more detailed views into the beginnings of time.

Einstein was born a German citizen but later became a Swiss citizen in 1901 and an American citizen in 1940.

Scientists, Mathematicians, and Engineers

Numerous astronomers, physicists, and astrophysicists contributed to the understanding of the big bang. Albert Einstein's work kicked off the theories of an expanding universe, but he himself did not believe in the big bang theory at first. The persistence of the big bang theory's supporters, and the discoveries they made, turned Einstein and the majority of the scientific community into believers.

ALBERT EINSTEIN

Albert Einstein, considered to be one of the greatest scientists in history, was born in Ulm, Germany, in 1879 and attended school in Munich. Contrary to popular belief, Einstein was an excellent student with an appetite for heavy books on science and mathematics. He disliked the teaching methodology in Munich, however, and after his family moved to Italy, Einstein left his high school in Munich and eventually resumed his education in Aurau, Switzerland.

Einstein attended the Swiss Federal Polytechnic School in Zurich, where he trained to be a teacher of physics and mathematics. He graduated in 1901 and, unable to find a teaching position, began working at the Swiss Patent Office. The role was dull, but he could quickly finish his official work and then turn to his own physics work. He was especially fond of using thought-experiments, in which he performed conceptual experiments to test theories that he could not test in the real world. In one famous example, sixteen-year-old Einstein imagined that he was riding a beam of light and watching another light beam move parallel to his. Classical physics suggested that the second light beam should move at a relative speed of zero, but if that was true, the laws of electromagnetism would then depend on the observer. Einstein believed the laws should be universal, and this thought-experiment formed the foundation of his special theory of relativity.

In 1905, after writing five papers on physics, including one on his special theory of relativity, Einstein obtained his doctoral degree. He became a professor at numerous universities in Europe, including in Bern, Zurich, Prague, and Berlin. In 1916, he published his paper on the general theory of relativity, which set the stage for the work of Georges Lemaître, Alexander Friedmann, and other big bang theorists.

In 1919, Cambridge scientist Sir Arthur Eddington tested Einstein's theory of general relativity using a total eclipse of the sun that provided an opportunity to test the effect of the sun's gravity on starlight. When the eclipse happened, Einstein's theory of gravity accurately accounted for the apparent position of stars behind the sun, whereas Newton's theory did not. "LIGHT ALL ASKEW IN THE HEAVENS," the *New York Times* headlines announced, "EINSTEIN'S THEORY TRIUMPHS." Einstein was now world-famous, a physics sensation. He made several trips to the United States to give speeches to packed audiences.

In 1933, Einstein renounced his German citizenship and moved to the United States, where he became a professor at Princeton University in New Jersey. Though Einstein was against war, his fear that the Germans would develop an atomic bomb first led him to sign a letter to President Roosevelt encouraging atomic bomb research.

Einstein loved to play the violin as well as the piano, which he often did as a form of relaxation and also as an aid to thinking through tough problems. After becoming famous as a physicist, he was often invited to play his violin at benefit concerts, which he did enthusiastically. One critic, unaware of Einstein's primary profession, said of his performance: "Einstein plays excellently. However, his worldwide fame is undeserved. There are many violinists who are just as good."

Einstein died in Princeton in 1955.

GEORGES LEMAÎTRE

Georges Lemaître has the unique distinction of being both a famous physicist and a Catholic priest, as well being the scientist who proposed the first version of the big bang theory.

Lemaître was born in 1894 in Charleroi, Belgium. He began university at the Catholic University of Louvain with the intent to become an engineer, but his studies were interrupted by World War I. He served an artillery officer and saw terrible carnage, including the first poison gas attack, and received the Military Cross for his bravery.

When the war was over, a troubled and changed Lemaître switched his major from engineering to theoretical physics and became an ordained priest in 1923. In 1924, he studied physics at Cambridge and later received a PhD in physics from the Massachusetts Institute of Technology (MIT).

In 1925, Lemaître became a professor of astrophysics at his alma mater, the Catholic University of Louvain in Belgium. Two years later, he published his theories on the expanding universe, which explained the recession of galaxies given Albert Einstein's theory of gravity. His idea was initially ignored until 1930, after Hubble's great discovery, when his old Cambridge professor Arthur Eddington began publicly promoting Lemaître's work. In a second paper in 1929, Lemaître introduced his theory of the "primeval atom" that exploded and decayed into space, time, and the expanding universe. In doing so, he launched the field of big bang cosmology.

Lemaître was determined to keep his religious beliefs separate from his study of physics and felt that a scientific theory of cosmology did not add to or interfere with his religious beliefs. "As far as I can see, such a theory remains entirely outside any metaphysical or religious question," he wrote.

Lemaître lived to see Einstein acclaim his work, Gamow and Alpher further the big bang theory (though their explanation of the initial seconds of the universe was much different than Lemaître's primeval atom theory), and Penzias and Wilson confirm the existence of the CMB.

In later years, Lemaître's work expanded to include papers on computer languages, calculating techniques, and computational mathematics. Lemaître died in 1966 in Belgium.

EDWIN HUBBLE

Edwin Hubble, the scientist who discovered that the Milky Way was not the only galaxy and that galaxies were moving away at speeds directly proportionate to their distance, was born in 1889 in Marshfield, Missouri. He attended the University of Chicago, where he studied mathematics and astronomy and participated in track, boxing, and basketball.

After graduating from the University of Chicago, he attended Oxford University as one of the first Rhodes Scholars. At Oxford, he studied Roman and English law instead of astronomy to please his father, and he set up a law practice in Louisville, Kentucky, in 1913. Knowing his true passion was in astronomy, however, he quickly changed course and obtained his PhD in astronomy at the University of Chicago.

When he finished his PhD in 1917, Hubble received a job offer from the Mount Wilson Observatory, the best observatory in the world at that time. However, immediately after finishing his PhD, Hubble enlisted in the military. "Regret cannot accept your invitation. Am off to the war," he telegraphed George Ellery Hale, the founder of the observatory and a leading astronomer.

When Hubble returned from the war, he took up the post at Mount Wilson Observatory. He served again in World War II at the Ballistics Research Laboratory at Aberdeen in Maryland, for which he won a Medal of Merit, before returning back to his research. After the war, he helped design the 200-inch (508-centimeter) Hale Telescope that would be placed at the new Mount Palomar Observatory to see further than ever before. He researched at both observatories until his death in 1953.

GEORGE GAMOW

George Gamow was born in Odessa in modern-day Ukraine. He was a curious young boy, and once put pieces of communion bread and wine under a microscope to compare them to regular bread and wine in search of the body of Christ.

He attended the Novorossia University in Odessa and then went to Leningrad to study with Alexander Friedmann, who was working on theories of an expanding universe. He researched natural radioactivity and the transformation of light elements and obtained his PhD from the University of Leningrad. He later worked at the Institute of Theoretical Physics for a year on a stipend from the Royal Danish Academy. While at the institute, he helped advance the understanding of nuclear fission and nuclear fusion.

Gamow spent a year at Cambridge University, followed by another year in Copenhagen, before becoming a professor at the University of Leningrad. His early achievements in nuclear science attracted favorable attention from a state-owned newspaper, but Gamow wanted to leave the Soviet Union. At the time, Soviet scientists could be forced by Soviet leaders to support outdated and disproven theories.

Gamow and his wife tried to escape three times, including in a kayak across the Black Sea to Turkey and across the Arctic Ocean to Norway. The third time, Gamow arranged for his wife, also a physicist, to accompany him to a physics conference in Brussels. They never returned to the Soviet Union. Instead, they moved to the United States, where Gamow took a position at George Washington University.

Gamow spent the next two decades dedicated to studying nucleosynthesis in relation to the big bang. No other nuclear scientist in the United States seemed to be working on this problem. It turned out that everyone else had been recruited to work on the Manhattan Project to design and build the first atomic bombs. Gamow had not been invited to join the team because he had once been a commissioned officer of the Red Army, though only as a teacher.

In the 1950s, Gamow began publishing papers on the storage and transfer of information in living cells, proposing a "genetic code" that was later confirmed in lab experiments. He also wrote a popular science fiction series titled "The Adventures of Mr. Tompkins" and many other popular science works. He died in 1968.

RALPH ALPHER

Ralph Alpher was born in Washington, DC, in 1921 and was a bright student. He was initially offered a full scholarship to the Massachusetts Institute of Technology, but the scholarship was withdrawn, he said, after he revealed that he was Jewish. Instead, Alpher attended George Washington University at night while working during the day.

Alpher's science career was, unfortunately, characterized by overlooked accomplishments. Alpher worked closely with his professor, George Gamow, to build the nucleosynthesis model of the big bang, predicting that the universe went from big bang to fusion within a five-minute window. Alpher later predicted that the expansion of the universe would have left detectable background radiation. When Gamow and

Alpher published their paper titled "The Origin of Chemical Elements," Gamow added his friend Hans Bethe's name to the paper. The authorship now read "Alpher Bethe Gamow," a play on the Greek letters alpha, beta, gamma. Alpher's name was overshadowed by the names of the older, more famous scientists, and his role in developing the big bang model and predicting the CMB was overlooked for decades.

Alpher left the field of cosmology in the 1950s, first working at General Electric's research and development center in Schenectady, New York, before becoming a research professor at Union College (also in Schenectady) in 1986.

In 2007, Alpher won the National Medal of Science "for his unprecedented work in the areas of nucleosynthesis" as well as his prediction of the CMB and development of the big bang theory. He died a month later.

FRED HOYLE

Fred Hoyle was a leading opponent of the big bang theory, but he contributed significantly to the theory nonetheless. Hoyle preferred the steady state theory of the universe, which he and his Cambridge colleagues Hermann Bondi and Thomas Gold had created in 1948.

In a BBC radio lecture in 1949, Hoyle referred to his opponents' model of the universe as a moment of creation "in one big bang." The phrase stuck, and to this day the expanding universe model is known as the big bang model of cosmology. Hoyle also developed the model of heavy element fusion within stars, which helped explain how heavy elements could exist in a big bang universe.

Hoyle was born in West Yorkshire in 1915, just before his father was conscripted into the British army and sent to fight in World War I. Hoyle was a bright student, though often truant in his early education, but his appetite for education grew over the years, and he devoted himself to self-study in order to obtain a scholarship to Cambridge. At Cambridge, Hoyle had world-famous instructors, including Max Born and Sir Arthur Eddington.

Hoyle later became a professor at Cambridge. He also gave a series of BBC radio lectures that were popular with the general public, wrote several science fiction novels, wrote a television series, and a children's play. In 1966 Hoyle founded the Institute of Theoretical Astronomy at Cambridge and served as director until 1972.

Hoyle was knighted and elected to many scientific academies and societies. He died in 2001.

ARNO PENZIAS

Arno Penzias, one of the two scientists who discovered the CMB, was born to a Jewish family in Munich in 1933. When he was a child, his family was deported to Poland. They made it back to Munich, and in the spring of 1939, his parents sent Penzias and his younger brother on a train to England. Their parents joined them there soon after, and the entire family made its way by ship to the United States in December 1939.

Penzias attended the City College of New York, the first free university in the United States designed to provide advanced education to children of immigrants and the poor. After graduating and serving two years in the US Army Signal Corps, Penzias obtained his PhD in physics at Columbia University in 1962. He focused extensively on radio astronomy, a new field at the time, before joining Bell Labs, where he could continue his work in the field.

A dash of luck helped set Penzias on his path to astrophysics fame when Bell Labs built an antenna for a satellite project. The antenna proved to be unnecessary and Penzias and his colleague Robert Wilson set out to use the antenna to study the radiation from the Milky Way. Instead, they found that the universe itself was radiating energy.

After the Nobel Prize-winning discovery of the big bang, Penzias used radio astronomy to study the molecular spectra of interstellar atoms. In doing so, he was able to trace the nuclear process that created those atoms. He also took leadership roles at Bell Labs while continuing his own research, advancing to become Vice President of Research. A few years before reaching Bell Labs' retirement cutoff, he left and joined the Silicon Valley startup and venture capital world.

ROBERT WILSON

Robert Wilson, Penzias's counterpart in discovering the cosmic microwave background radiation (CMB) at Bell Labs, was born in January 1936 in Houston, where his father worked for an oil company. Wilson grew up with an interest in electronics, fixing radios and television sets and building his own radios. He attended Rice University, where he studied physics and worked a summer job at Exxon (an oil company). There he obtained his first patent.

Wilson went on to Caltech, and he earned his PhD in physics with a focus on radio astronomy. In 1963, Wilson began at Bell Labs, where he worked with the organization's only other radio astronomer, Arno Penzias.

GEORGE SMOOT

George Smoot, the lead scientist behind the COBE satellite and the discovery of fluctuations in the CMB, was born in Yukon, Florida, in 1945. He first became interested in astronomy as a young child on a road trip across Alabama. The moon seemed to be following the family's car, and young Smoot asked his parents how it knew to follow them. His parents gave him a quick lesson in distance and perspective, and Smoot was impressed by how the beauty he saw in the world could be understood through evaluation.

Education was very important to the family. Smoot's mother, who had a master's degree in science education, taught

Smoot supplementary science while he was in high school, and his engineer father drilled him in mathematics. Smoot attended MIT for his undergraduate degrees in mathematics and physics and his PhD in physics. At the age of twenty-five, he started his career at the University of California at Berkeley, which had many Nobel Laureate researchers. His first project was the NASA-funded High-Altitude Particle Physics Experiment, which originally aimed to study high-energy particle reactions and later shifted to focus on finding evidence for the big bang.

In 1973, Smoot began to focus on finding fluctuations in the CMB. With support from Berkeley and NASA, Smoot's team developed a differential microwave radiometer that could measure the differences in temperature in microwave radiation between two points. Eventually, one of Smoot's instruments went up in the COBE satellite that his team launched in a NASA rocket in 1989, which gathered the first evidence of fluctuations in the CMB. Smoot won the Nobel Prize in Physics in 2006 for his discoveries supporting the big bang model of cosmology.

THE TECHNOLOGY BEHIND THE BIG BANG THEORY

Developing a theory of the big bang was only possible because of the technology available. Without telescopes, spectroscopes, photography, and satellites, scientists would be blind to the events that took place billions of years ago.

Spectroscopes and Spectrographs

One of the first major technological advancements in studying the early history of the universe is the spectroscope, a device that measures light spectra. Spectroscopes provide astronomers with a way to study light spectra, which can tell both the chemical composition of an object as well as its **radial velocity** away from our vantage point on Earth.

Today, more advanced devices called spectrographs split light into its component wavelengths using either a prism or, more commonly, through diffraction grating. (Prisms absorb some of the light that passes through, whereas diffraction gratings do not.) A prism is usually made of glass and refracts (bends) light while a diffraction grating spectroscope uses thousands of lines carved into a glass surface to reflect light. If you have ever seen a rainbow on the surface of a CD, you have seen a diffraction grating. Another advantage of diffraction gratings is that they can reflect ultraviolet (UV) light, whereas a glass prism cannot.

Red light has a longer wavelength than blue light, which causes it to bend much less as it passes through a spectroscope. The different refraction (in prisms) or reflection (in diffraction gratings) angles of each color of light produces a rainbow. Today, spectroscopes can capture light at all portions of the electromagnetic spectrum, from infrared to X-ray and gamma ray radiation.

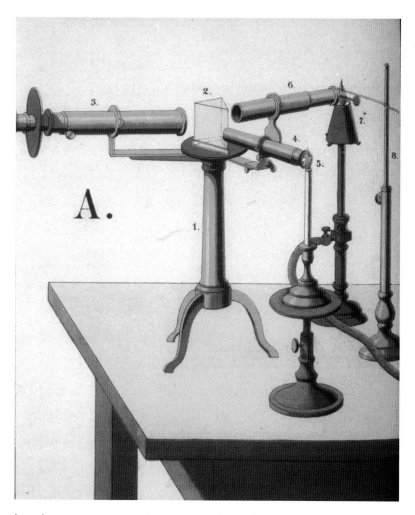

In early spectroscopes, a scale was projected onto the spectral image to allow scientists to measure the lines.

Originally, astronomical spectra were often photographed onto glass plates, which provided an easy way for astronomers to create a spectrum and preserve it for future analysis. These spectra were often compared to the spectra from a lamp light with a known spectra. In modern spectrographs, spectra can be recorded digitally.

Photography

Newton's gravity theory also predicted a shift in light, but only by half as much as Einstein's theory.

Astronomers were early adopters of photography when it was first announced by Daguerre (creator of the daguerreotype) in 1839. By 1840, John W. Draper had taken the first photo of the moon, and the first photo of the sun came five years later. In 1851, scientists took a photo of a total eclipse of the sun, a process that would be an important part of proving Einstein's theory of general relativity correct in 1919.

That year, Sir Arthur Eddington led a team to the Gulf of Guinea off the west coast of Africa and sent a second team to Brazil to take photos of stars visible due to the darkness of a solar eclipse. The sun was passing in front of the Hyades star cluster at that time, and during the eclipse, the stars appeared shifted in the sky because their light was bent by the mass of the sun. Einstein's general theory of relativity accurately predicted this effect, and the solar eclipse test effectively proved him right. As scientists dug deeper into the general theory of relativity, which in its original form suggested the universe must be either contracting or expanding, the big bang theory was born.

Photography was also part of Hubble's method in measuring the distance to far-off galaxies and is a now a standard tool in astronomy.

The Hooker Space Telescope

The Hooker Space Telescope has been called the most important telescope of the twentieth century because, with Edwin Hubble at the eyepiece, it brought about some of the most significant changes in our understanding of the universe.

The Hooker Space Telescope was the largest telescope in the world at the time it was built. It had a 100-inch (254 cm) glass disc that reflected light and could be used for both photography and spectroscopy. The size of a telescope's mirror determines how much light it can collect and thus how far off into space it can "see." When the disk was made, it was a feat of glasswork, and it took several tries to get a disk that large to meet the right standards of quality. It was also an expensive project and was funded by a Los Angeles businessman named John D. Hooker, who was willing to pay

Transporting the components of the Hooker Telescope up Mount Wilson required a widened road, a custom truck, and eventually, mules.

for the telescope in exchange for having the world's largest telescope bear his name.

The telescope includes an eyepiece with crosshairs, which the telescope's operator had to keep precisely focused on the object of study (such as a single star) for as long as eight hours

The Big Bang Theory and Light Spectra

back when the Hooker Telescope was used by professionals. At that time, the telescope had glass plates with layers of light-sensitive colloids (chemical mixtures) on them that, over the observation time, would develop into photographs on the plates.

The Hooker Space Telescope is part of the Mount Wilson Observatory, located on a mountain with exceptionally clear skies due to steady winds that lifted ocean-cooled air over the peak. Today, the telescope is not used for professional research but is available for public use.

The Large Horn Antenna

The Large Horn Antenna in Holmdel, New Jersey, is one of the more unique instruments used to find evidence in support of the big bang model. The antenna was originally built to be part of a communications satellite project, but when the project was ready to launch, the antenna turned out to be unnecessary. Instead, Bell Labs' two radio astronomers, Arno Penzias and Robert Wilson, were allowed to use the antenna in their research, which led to the discovery of the CMB.

The Large Horn Antenna is a relatively massive metal object, weighing in at 18 tons (36,000 pounds). The aluminum antenna is 20 feet (6 meters) long and is surrounded by a horn that directs radio waves to the antenna. The radio receiver is cooled with liquid helium, which helps reduce interference (as heat produces radiation). The horn

The Perot Museum's Expanding Universe Hall

The Perot Museum of Nature and Science in Dallas has a 2,200-square-foot (204-square-meter) interactive exhibit dedicated to the big bang and the expansion of the universe.

The Expanding Universe Hall includes a 3D dome where visitors can watch a big bang simulation, images of space taken by the Hubble Space Telescope, and a 3D trip through our solar system. Visitors can also learn about the physics of the big bang and the expanding universe through interactive explorations into topics such as light spectra and spectrum analysis and different types of matter. Selfie-snapping underneath a floating astronaut is encouraged.

The Perot Museum is located inside a modern building that opened in December 2012. The building, which includes environmental features such as an acre of rocks and grasses on the rooftop, obtained an LEED gold rating from the US Green Building Council for its sustainable building design. The Perot Museum was funded entirely by donations, including a large donation from the children of Ross and Margot Perot, for whom the museum is named.

The museum also includes permanent exhibits featuring dinosaurs, DNA, robots, wacky weather, and more.

When the Large Horn Antenna is not in use, it is allowed to find a position of minimum wind resistance, like a weathervane.

is connected to a wheel on a base frame, 30 feet (9.1 m) in diameter, that rotates and aims the antenna at different positions in the sky.

The COBE Satellite

The Cosmic Background Explorer (COBE) satellite launched in 1989 in pursuit of measurements of the CMB. It contained three instruments, including a Differential Microwave Radiometer (DMR) that used horn antennas aimed 60 degrees apart to detect small temperature variations between different parts of the sky.

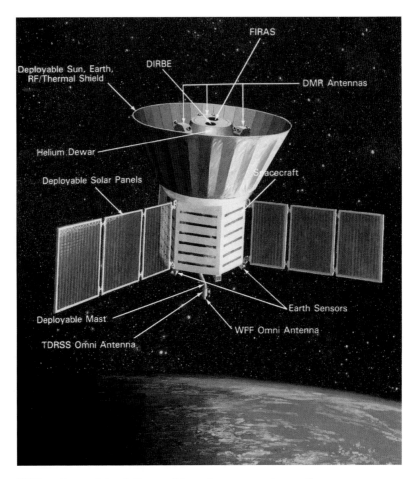

COBE could complete a full scan of the universe every six months.

Over the period of several years in space, COBE sent back precise measurements of the diffuse infrared and microwave radiation in the universe. The DMR was the most important part of COBE in relation to the big bang theory, as it detected the variations in the CMB over the entire sky. These fluctuations in the radiation's intensity are thought to be the seeds that, over time and under the effect of gravity, would separate into clumps of matter and eventually become galaxies and large scale structures in the universe.

IMAGING THE BIG BANG ITSELF

All of the instruments mentioned above capture data from the time the universe was several hundreds of thousands of years old and older. No instruments to date have been able to look earlier than that time period. It is here that simulations become significant. When it comes to big bang research, that primarily means simulations of the early universe conducted in particle accelerators.

CERN's Large Hadron Collider focuses on studying the conditions of the infant universe to learn where matter came from.

Visualizing the
Big Bang Theory

Astronomers can take a look far back in time by looking at galaxies billions of light years away. Due to the time it takes for their light to reach us here on Earth, we see those galaxies as they were billions of years ago, giving insight into the conditions of a younger universe.

But back before 380,000 years post-big bang, the conditions of the early universe were such that light was scattered everywhere and the universe was opaque. Those earliest years, and especially the moments of the big bang and the seconds before it, are beyond our current observational abilities. (Observations like the expansion of the universe and the CMB provide support for the big bang theory but do not prove it happened.)

If scientists could see those first seconds, days, and years, however, they would provide direct evidence for or against the big bang. Observing those early moments would help physicists understand the laws of physics that operated in the extreme conditions of the big bang. As it is today, the laws of physics as we know them (a topic discussed further in the next chapter) break down in conditions so hot and highly energetic.

How, then, can scientists study the big bang and the earliest moments of the universe?

Einstein turned to thought-experiments to delve into the unknown universe. George Gamow and Ralph Alpher used mathematics and the process of nucleosynthesis to develop their early model of the big bang. Today, physicists use enormous, high-energy particle accelerators to replicate the conditions immediately following the big bang.

PARTICLE ACCELERATORS

Particle accelerators are machines that use electromagnetic fields and other mechanisms to bring particles such as protons to extremely high velocities. Physicists typically put the fast-moving particles on collision paths in order to research the effects of those collisions or, in some cases, to generate high energy rays.

The acceleration increases the energy of the particles. Because of this, particle accelerators provide an opportunity to study the conditions of the early universe immediately after the big bang when the universe was hot, dense, and filled with very intense energy. Upon collision, the accelerated, high

Fermilab's discoveries include fundamental particles such as the Higgs boson (in collaboration with CERN) and the top and bottom quarks.

energy particles break apart and new, often rare, particles form. Physicists then analyze the data they gather from those collisions and observe what happens to particles under those highly energetic conditions.

Today, there are more than thirty thousand particle accelerators in the world, and they fall into two primary shapes: circular and linear. A circular accelerator is shaped like a ring and particles travel around the ring. A linear accelerator is built in a straight line and a beam of particles travels from one end to the other.

In general, the longer the path of the particle, the faster the particle will accelerate. Large particle accelerators, such as the Fermilab accelerator in Illinois and the Large

Visualizing the Big Bang Theory

Hadron Collider in Switzerland and France, are usually built underground to minimize the cost of building such large structures above ground. Being underground also protects the accelerators from external interference.

Many accelerators are dedicated to physics research, but there are other uses as well. For example, hospitals use linear accelerators to produce and deliver radiation therapy for patients with cancer. Pharmaceutical research and development scientists use accelerators to create powerful X-rays that image protein crystals while creating new drugs.

Early Accelerators

The first particle accelerator was built in 1930 when physicist Ernest Lawrence and graduate student M. Stanley Livingston, both at the University of California at Berkeley, developed an accelerator with a chamber just under 5 inches (12.7 cm) across. Lawrence designed the accelerator, called a cyclotron, to learn more about the atomic nucleus, which Ernest Rutherford had discovered in 1911. Bringing particles to higher energy levels would allow physicists to break apart, transform, and better understand nuclei. His graduate student, Livingston, was tasked with turning Lawrence's design into a working device as his PhD thesis.

The first cyclotron worked like a swing that moved particles back and forth along a spiral path, using electrodes that pushed and pulled ions faster and faster with each cycle.

Using that first model, Lawrence and Livingston were able to accelerate hydrogen ions up to energies of 80,000 electron volts (eV).

Electron volts are a measure of energy and 1 eV is equivalent to 1.6022×10^{-19} joules. In the grand scheme of things, an electron volt is a tiny amount of energy. A flying mosquito, for example, expends about 1 trillion eV, or 1 teraelectron volt (TeV). When that much energy is in a tiny particle, however, the energy density is so great that the collisions can break particles apart and create new particles.

Lawrence and Livingston soon built bigger particle accelerators, including a second cyclotron in 1931 that accelerated particles to 1 million eV. They started a lab dedicated to particle accelerators called the Radiation Laboratory of the University of California (today the Lawrence Berkeley National Laboratory). In 1939, Lawrence won the Nobel Prize in Physics for his work on cyclotrons. Throughout the 1930s and onward, scientists at other institutions also developed particle accelerators and made discoveries in atomic nuclei and radioactivity.

The Large Hadron Collider

The Large Hadron Collider (LHC) is the world's largest and most powerful particle accelerator. The LHC was built between 1998 and 2008 by the European Organization for Nuclear Research (CERN). It lies inside of a 16.5-mile

Rutherford and the Atomic Nucleus

Particle accelerators and big bang cosmology are both supported by an understanding of the atom and its component parts. The nucleus was discovered just over 100 years ago by British physicist Ernest Rutherford.

Prior to Rutherford's work, the common belief was that an atom was made up of a uniform, positive substance with embedded electrons. In 1909, Rutherford suggested that an undergraduate student looking for a research project study the effects of shooting alpha particles (positive helium ions) at gold foil. The alpha particles were emitted through a slit in a lead screen and concentrated on a piece of gold foil. Another screen coated with zinc sulfide was used to track the movement of the alpha particles. When a particle hit the zinc sulfide screen, it would produce light.

Most of the particles passed through the gold foil, which suggested that the gold atoms were mostly made up of open space that could allow particles to pass through. Some of the particles, however, bounced off the gold foil at large angles. This indicated that the positive alpha particles had hit dense, positively charged particles in the gold atoms and were repelled. Because only a small portion of the alpha particles bounced back, this positively charged component of the atom (the nucleus) must be very small compared to the size of the entire atom. From this experiment, Rutherford put together a model with light, negative electrons orbiting a tiny, positive nucleus.

Rutherford's work made way for the particle accelerators of the 1930s and the future of particle physics. Rutherford himself called for scientists to develop new ways to bring particles up to higher energies to study the newly discovered atomic nucleus. Physicist Ernest Lawrence at Berkeley, designer of the first particle accelerator, was one of the scientists who rose to Rutherford's challenge.

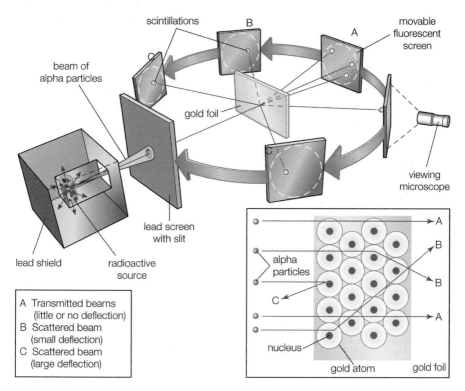

scintillations

B

A

movable fluorescent screen

beam of alpha particles

gold foil

lead screen with slit

viewing microscope

lead shield

radioactive source

A Transmitted beams (little or no deflection)
B Scattered beam (small deflection)
C Scattered beam (large deflection)

alpha particles

nucleus

gold atom

gold foil

Rutherford compared the results of the gold foil experiment to a bullet fired at tissue paper that "came back and hit you."

(27 km) circular tunnel buried beneath Switzerland and France near Geneva. It is certainly not the only accelerator of note (Fermilab in the United States, for example, has contributed a great deal to particle physics), but it is the primary accelerator investigating the big bang.

Inside, the accelerator has a region that uses a positively charged electric field to remove the electrons from nuclei. Another region has a negatively charged electric field that attracts the protons and moves them forward. (The charge pulsates so that the protons move forward in bunches rather than a steady stream).

These quadrupole magnets, designed and built at Fermilab for CERN, focus proton beams at interaction regions to maximize particle collisions.

Throughout the accelerator, there are chambers that resonate at radio frequencies. When a particle bunch moves through a radiofrequency chamber, the radio waves interact with the particles and transfer some of their energy to the particles. One way to imagine this energy is to visualize a surfer catching an ocean wave. On a flat ocean, the surfer has a small amount of energy and moves slowly. When riding a wave, the surfer has much greater, more (metaphorically) explosive energy and moves faster. In a similar way, the particles gain energy and velocity from their interactions with the radio waves.

Very strong magnets bend and focus the particles by creating a magnetic field that changes the path of the particles to go around the ring. While the accelerator looks circular from above, in actuality, the particles follow a straight line that bends in dozens of places to create the effect of a circle on a large scale. **Dipole magnets**, the type of magnets with opposing north and south poles, take care of bending the path of the particles into a circle parallel to the ground while **quadrupole magnets**, which have two sets of north and south poles arranged in an "X" pattern, focus the beam by gathering the particles together. In order to conduct electricity without any resistance, the magnets are cooled down to -456.3 degrees Fahrenheit (-271.3 °C), a few degrees colder than outer space.

The particles move through a vacuum, which ensures that particles do not collide with any gas molecules as they accelerate. Throughout the accelerator, there are also four particle detectors near the collision sites that measure what happens when a particle collides with another beam of particles. The detectors include ATLAS and CMS, two general purpose detectors; ALICE, a detector that studies a type of plasma created by the big bang; and LHCb, a detector investigating matter and antimatter in the early universe.

The first particle accelerator built by Lawrence and Livingston accelerated hydrogen ions up to 80,000 eV. Today,

A Higgs boson is produced before decaying into jets of hadrons and electrons. The visualization's lines represent possible particle paths; the blue regions represent energy.

the LHC can accelerate protons up to 6.5 trillion electron volts (TeV) for a total collision energy of 13 TeV.

One recent experiment at the LHC focused on that early universe plasma. It is thought that just after the big bang, the universe was filled with a hot, dense, soup made up of what is called quark-gluon plasma. In 2016, CERN researchers collided positively charged lead ions at energies twice as high as any previous LHC experiment in order to simulate the quark-gluon plasma.

The energy of the collision created a quark-gluon plasma over 100,000 times hotter than the sun, with particles moving at nearly the speed of light. The particles were primarily quarks, the building blocks of protons and neutrons; and gluons, the particles that carry the strong nuclear force and bind quarks together. After analysis, researchers found that the quark-gluon plasma behaved more like a fluid than a gas. This was the opposite of what physicists expected to find. They also were able to study the debris that formed as the quark-gluon plasma quickly cooled down and created particles of ordinary matter, including protons and neutrons.

After any particle collision, there will be an immense amount of data from the particle detectors. At the LHC, this can be around 30 petabytes (30 x 109 megabytes) of data that is sent to the CERN Data Centre and digitally reconstructed. (It's estimated that just one petabyte of data could store enough MP3 files to create a two-thousand-year-long playlist.) Supercomputers help process that huge amount of data so physicists have near real-time access to their LHC data.

The Future of Particle Accelerators

Particle accelerators are just under ninety years old, significantly younger than telescopes, spectroscopy, photography, and other technology used to study the big bang and cosmic inflation. They are getting continually bigger and crashing particles at continually higher energies. Physicists hope that higher-energy collisions will provide a better opportunity to discover new particles and learn more about the early physics of our universe.

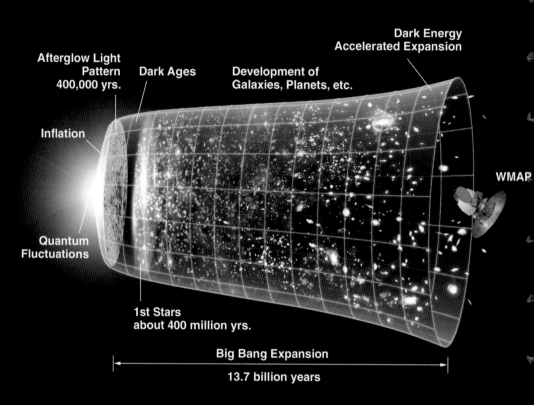

Afterglow Light
Pattern
400,000 yrs.

Dark Ages

Development of
Galaxies, Planets, etc.

Dark Energy
Accelerated Expansion

Inflation

Quantum
Fluctuations

1st Stars
about 400 million yrs.

Big Bang Expansion

13.7 billion years

WMAP

Scientists don't yet know how to obtain direct data from the (literal) dark ages between the CMB and the emergence of stars.

5

The Big Bang Theory Today and Tomorrow

In the scientific community, it is largely agreed upon that the big bang model of cosmology will continue to be modified, updated, and expanded. However, the general theory is expected to stand the test of time. There are still many unanswered questions around the beginning of the universe. Current research examines some of these questions, such as what caused the rapid cosmic inflation in the first fraction of a second, how the laws of physics operated in that moment, and how to detect neutrinos created by the big bang. Others are unanswerable with our current knowledge and scientific tools, such as what came before the big bang.

COSMIC INFLATION

In 1980, the physicist Alan Guth modified the original big bang theory of Gamow and Alpher. Guth suggested that the universe didn't begin as an actual fiery explosion but as a rapid inflation of a tiny region of space into a vast universe. The enormous growth spurt, which Guth said was due to a repulsive gravity created by negative pressures, took place in just a fraction of a second—in the first billionth of a trillionth of a trillionth of a trillionth of a second of the universe's life.

The inflationary model explains a number of properties of the universe. For example, the homogeneity and relative smoothness of the CMB throughout the entire universe suggests that at one point the entire universe was connected, despite the vast distance between points. If the far edges of the universe had never been in contact with one another, scientists wonder, could the universe have come to equilibrium at the same temperature across such a vast distance? If the universe had expanded very quickly after the big bang, this could help explain how far-off regions are so similar.

Another reason why scientists believe that inflation happened is because our universe is very close to perfectly flat. To understand why this measurement is important, consider a bowling ball. It must move very fast down the bowling alley to stay perfectly in the center of the lane. If the ball moves slowly, any slight variation in how the ball started moving will become amplified, and the bowling ball will end up in the gutter. Similarly, if gravity is the only force affecting an expanding universe, it is unlikely to stay flat as it grows, even if it was perfectly flat when it started. Nonetheless, ours did stay very flat. Just as the speed of the bowling ball can keep the bowling ball perfectly in the middle, the intense speed of inflation preserved the subatomic smoothness and flatness present in the tiny, early universe and expanded it to the enormous universe we know today.

When Einstein came up with the theory of general relativity, he added an anti-gravity cosmological constant to force the equations to predict a static universe. He later dismissed the cosmological constant when Hubble showed that the universe was expanding, but he may have been on to something. The cosmological constant can also describe the expansion for inflation, as well as the expansion caused by **dark energy**. Under this model, empty space has an energy that drives the expansion of the universe.

LAWS OF PHYSICS

There are four fundamental forces of nature in the universe. Gravity, the best-known force, keeps our feet on the ground and planets in orbit around the sun. The electromagnetic force determines the structure of atoms and the behavior of light. The two remaining forces are the weak nuclear force, which determines how subatomic particles radioactively decay and initiates stellar nuclear fusion; and the strong force, which binds quarks together into protons and neutrons and other subatomic particles and holds the atomic nucleus together.

Searching for Gravitational Waves

If inflation happened as many think it did, the violence of the rapid expansion should have sent gravitational waves rippling through space-time. As gravitational waves move through the universe, they distort space-time, specifically the radiation known as CMB.

In 2014, a team of researchers thought that they had found evidence of gravitational waves in the CMB and thus the first strong evidence for cosmic inflation. The results were part of the Background Imaging of Cosmic Extragalactic Polarization 2 (BICEP2) at the South Pole. The BICEP2 detector discovered a swirling pattern in the CMB that can only come from inflation, the team said. However, when the BICEP2 team combined their data with the data from other experiments, they found that it was most likely that the swirling pattern they found was produced by galactic dust inside the Milky Way.

In 2016, scientists announced BICEP3, which will comb the sky for the same type of evidence. BICEP3 has more detectors and more pixels and, by combining with a series of telescopes called the Keck Array, covers a wider spectrum of light, which the team hopes will allow it to see beyond the galactic dust and into the cosmic microwave background. Gravitational waves from other sources have been detected, but at this point, none have been detected from the big bang.

Einstein's theories predicted that massive events would cause ripples in space-time. Gravitational waves (from colliding black holes) were first detected in 2015.

Laws of physics that govern gravity and the observable universe are called classical physics. For example, general relativity predicts how gravity will work. Other laws of classical physics include the Law of the Conservation of Angular Momentum and Newton's Laws of Motion. Quantum mechanics govern the other three forces and determine how particles work, including atoms, photons, and quarks.

General relativity and quantum field theory (the theoretical framework that focuses on the strong, weak, and electromagnetic forces) are incompatible. General relativity accurately describes large-scale interactions. Quantum field theory accurately describes very small interactions between particles. The incompatibility shows itself when interactions take place in an extremely small but high-mass region. These conditions are found in black holes and the moment of the big bang. Our current physics can only explain what takes place after the first 10^{-43} seconds post-big bang.

The initial era in which our physics break down due to the extreme conditions is known as the **Planck era**. It is thought by many scientists that in the Planck era, all four fundamental forces of nature should unite in what is known as the theory of everything. When (and if) scientists discover this unified theory, they expect to have much more insight into what happened during the Planck era. (Einstein dedicated the last three decades of his life to finding a theory of everything that could unite the classical laws with the quantum laws.)

Einstein did not find a theory of everything, but one possible answer is **string theory**. String theory proposes that the fundamental units are not particles but tiny one-dimensional, vibrating strings of energy. When the strings vibrate in different patterns, they produce different kinds of particles. The math behind string theory supports both quantum mechanics and general relativity (given multiple, theoretical extra dimensions), but none of the predictions it makes are testable at this time.

Researchers have been able to use string theory mathematics to solve problems in condensed matter physics, such as superconductors, however. Some scientists, including theoretical physicist Edward Witten, believe that if string theory can be successfully applied to some physics fields, it indicates that it can be applied to other, deeper fields of physics as well.

After the Planck era, which lasted from 0 to 10^{-43} seconds, scientists believe that the strong, weak, and electromagnetic forces were united in what is known as the grand unified theory or the GUT era. The strong force separated around 10^{-35} seconds, releasing a huge amount of energy. The electromagnetic force and weak force remained combined until about 10^{-12} seconds, after which point the universe was governed by the separate physical laws as we know them now.

Physicists across the world are searching for evidence of this procession of the early universe. One supporting discovery in recent years is the Higgs boson particle, predicted and subsequently confirmed to exist in the LHC at CERN in 2014. The Higgs boson is thought to be the only particle present during the GUT era.

The LHC can be used to simulate the instant after the big bang, but it has limitations for explaining the very earliest moments of the universe. To produce energies similar to the state of the universe at 10^{-38} seconds after the big bang, scientists would have to create energies a trillion times larger than is currently possible with the LHC.

MATTER AND ANTIMATTER

Another one of the great mysteries of physics and the big bang is the asymmetry in matter and antimatter. The big bang should have created the same amount of matter and antimatter. In a perfectly symmetrical arrangement, the matter and antimatter would have annihilated each other completely. The universe would have nothing but the energy left over from those annihilations. Instead, physicists estimate that one particle per billion particles of matter survived. What caused this asymmetry?

Scientists at the LHC are searching for a cause to this imbalance, as are a team of scientists in Japan at the SuperKEKB particle accelerator. Both teams will study what happens when matter and antimatter particles are created in high energy collisions. Differences in how particles and antiparticles decay could explain the asymmetry.

BIG BANG NEUTRINOS

The energy of the big bang created all of the known particles, including protons, neutrons, and electrons. Physicists think the big bang also created a subatomic particle called a neutrino. A neutrino is a weakly interacting particle with no electric charge that is produced by the decay of radioactive elements and nuclear reactions.

Other types of neutrinos are produced by the birth, collisions, and death of stars, as well as by nuclear bombs,

IceCube includes about five thousand cold-hardy sensors spaced on strings and buried beneath the ice.

particle accelerators, and other sources. Most neutrinos, however, are thought to come from the moments immediately after the big bang before the creation of light elements. By studying these neutrinos, physicists hope to learn more about the universe in those early moments, such as how matter is distributed throughout the universe.

Neutrinos are incredibly light and they move at nearly the speed of light. Because they are weakly interacting, they can travel through the universe and Earth's atmosphere without interference. (It is estimated that each one of us has 10,000,000 neutrinos from the big bang passing through our bodies at any given moment!) This also makes neutrinos particularly hard to detect, however.

Physicists have been able to detect solar neutrinos by building detectors that look for neutrino energy transfers or neutrino transformations. The detectors are massive so that they can capture enough neutrinos to have a chance of observing one interact. (In the University of Minnesota's Soudan Underground Laboratory, more than one trillion man-made neutrinos pass through the lab's detector each year, but only 1,500 of those neutrinos will collide with atoms in the detector.) Detectors are typically built far underground, such as the IceCube Neutrino Observatory buried underneath ice in the South Pole (led by the University of Wisconsin-Madison) and the Soudan Underground Laboratory buried 2,341 feet (713.5 m) beneath the ground in an old Minnesota iron mine. The neutrinos from the big bang have much lower energies and are even harder to detect. (In fact, none have been detected so far.)

A group of physicists at the Princeton Plasma Physics Laboratory (a lab managed by the US Department of Energy) are on the hunt for big bang neutrinos as of summer 2016. The project, called PTOLEMY, uses tritium, a radioactive isotope of hydrogen that can capture neutrinos. As the tritium decays, the neutrinos would provide a small boost of energy to the electrons emitted in that decay. Superconducting magnets guide the electrons through PTOLEMY's detector, and a calorimeter measures their energy. The current setup is a prototype, and the team aims to detect big bang neutrinos, measure their mass, and eventually build a much larger experiment.

THE GOLDILOCKS CONUNDRUM

Why were the conditions of the early universe precisely such that the universe was filled with matter that formed into galaxies and stars and sustained life? Just like the story *Goldilocks and the Three Bears*, in which Goldilocks tests porridge, chairs, and beds to find just the right temperatures and sizes, physicists often wonder why the universe had just the right conditions to bring us to where we are today.

The conditions of the early universe were very precisely right for life. The variation between temperatures in the CMB, for example, is about 10^{-5} K. If the temperature variations were smaller, the clumps of dark matter (the substance that clumped first and attracted ordinary matter to form galaxies) would have produced galaxies with inefficient star systems and no planetary systems. If the temperature variations were greater than 10^{-5} K, the fluctuations would have been so strong that matter would have condensed into enormous structures that collapsed into supermassive black holes. Neither option could sustain life.

Similarly, a small deviation in any direction in the strong nuclear force value (which binds protons and neutrons together to form nuclei) would have had drastic consequences for the possibility of life. The strong nuclear force value is measured at 0.007. If it had been at 0.006, the reactions that fuse hydrogen into helium could not have taken place and stars would not have fuel. There would be no sunshine or photosynthesis or life. If the value was 0.008, the repulsion of the two hydrogen protons in the proton-proton fusion cycle would be overcome. The protons would bind together and the stars would have no hydrogen to burn. Again, life would not exist.

One common view in cosmology holds that perhaps there are other universes out there (such as in the **multiverse** scenario) and those that do not have the right conditions to sustain life do not have beings who contemplate the conditions of the universe. Only those universes that randomly have just the right conditions have living beings that contemplate the conditions of the universe. The universes that don't have the right conditions do not survive. The lucky ones that did, beyond our own, have different laws of physics and different contents.

RESEARCH OBSTACLES

One of the biggest challenges in big bang research is our inability to see back to the moment that it happened. Our most powerful telescopes can look back about 13 billion years, or between 400 and 800 million years post-big bang. (The farthest galaxy detected as of February 2016 is the EGS8p7 galaxy, more than 13.2 billion light years away.) NASA hopes that the James Webb Space Telescope will be able to look back to just 200 million years after the big bang to study the formation of the first galaxies, but this too leaves a large gap between the big bang and the beginning of the observable universe.

Technology isn't the only limiting factor to observing the big bang, however. Even if our telescopes could see 13.77 billion years ago to the moment the universe rapidly inflated from a small speck, it would be incredibly difficult to see what was happening. After the big bang, the universe was a hot soup of particles including free electrons, which scattered light and blocked it from traveling freely. With our current forms of technology, even if we advanced the power of the telescopes, we would not be able to see back beyond the era of recombination, or the time when neutral atoms formed and light could finally travel freely and the universe became visible. It is this period we look to when we study the CMB.

As a result, it is common for physicists to first theorize a change to our current big bang model and then seek ways to test or support that modification. Sometimes studying the CMB for signs of earlier events can be a way to support a modification of the currently accepted big bang theory. Relic neutrinos may provide information about particles and matter in the universe. At other times, physicists turn to particle accelerators to try to recreate the conditions and particles of the early universe to show that a theory is supported by experimental research.

BEFORE THE BIG BANG

One of the intriguing questions around the big bang is "What came before the big bang?" In some cosmological models, this is a redundant question, as the big bang is the moment in which space and time appeared. There is no time before the big bang if the big bang is the beginning of time itself. Some say that talking about time before the big bang was like talking about a region north of the North Pole. It doesn't exist, and it isn't logical to discuss it.

The real trouble, however, is that we don't have the scientific understanding to knowledgeably predict what happened before the big bang. Our cosmological model and our understanding of space-time is based on Einstein's theory of general relativity. Our understanding of the early universe is governed by quantum mechanics. We don't know, however, what described the conditions before (or even immediately after) the big bang. Our rules don't work. Our conceptions of space and time don't make sense.

Increasingly, however, physicists believe that there was something before the big bang that gave rise to the big

Scientists are looking for impact marks on the CMB that could show evidence of collisions with other bubbles in a hypothetical multiverse.

expansion. One theory, the bubble universe theory, states that our universe is just a fraction of all that exists, one bubble among many others. According to this theory, in the beginning there was a vacuum simmering with dark energy (which is also the unknown force causing the universe to accelerate increasingly fast) that eventually evaporated and formed bubbles. The dark energy caused the bubbles to expand and create multiple universes, or a multiverse. There were many cosmic expansions before our own, and there will be many cosmic expansions after our own.

A possibly frustrating reality of asking "What came before the big bang?" is that even when we arrive at a scientifically supported answer, we then have a new time horizon to consider. If we know what era came before the big bang, what came before that era? The quest for "What came before" is likely to never have a final, satisfying answer.

A FEW ANSWERS AND MANY QUESTIONS

Scientists are constantly working to build telescopes that can take in more light and thus analyze light from farther across the universe and farther back in time.

Developing a more accurate model of the origins of the universe and how physics worked in those early moments may never impact the ordinary person's daily life. Knowing how the first second unfolded and what happened in the dark years that followed does not change how we get to school, eat our dinner, or go to sleep. And yet, these answers address the biggest questions of all, and for some, that knowledge is life changing.

How did the universe begin? Why is the universe the way it is? What more is there to learn from light and energy? Over the past centuries, taking a scientific approach to these questions has brought scientists closer to understanding the origins of the universe.

Glossary

antiparticle A subatomic particle that has the same mass as a given corresponding particle but the opposite charge.

blackbody An object that absorbs and emits all wavelengths of light, producing a continuous spectrum. As temperature increases, the amount of light produced increases and peak wavelength decreases.

blueshift The shift of a galaxy or other object's emitted light toward bluer (shorter) wavelengths because the object is moving through space toward the observer.

cosmic microwave background The thermal radiation leftover from the big bang that can be found uniformly throughout the universe. Today, this radiation has cooled and stretched to microwave wavelengths.

cosmological constant In cosmology, the value of the energy density of the vacuum of space that is responsible for the accelerating expansion of the universe. Einstein added a cosmological constant to this theory of general relativity to force it to predict a static universe.

dark energy The mysterious force that propels the expansion of the universe.

dark matter The unknown, nonluminous matter that makes up most of the matter in the universe.

decoupling The process in which, about 240,000 to 300,000 years after the big bang, photons separated from matter and traveled freely through the universe.

dipole magnet A magnet with opposite poles, such as north and south poles, on opposite sides of the magnet.

electromagnetic spectrum The entire range of wavelengths or frequencies of radiation, from gamma rays to radio waves.

electron volt A unit of energy; 1 eV equals 1.6022×10^{-19} joules.

Hubble Constant The expansion rate of the universe, measured at 73.8 kilometers per second per megaparsec. (A megaparsec is a distance of 3.26 million light years.)

infrared The portion of the electromagnetic spectrum with a wavelength just longer than the red end of the visible light spectrum but shorter than the microwave portion of the spectrum.

intrinsic luminosity The total amount of energy a star radiates each second; the absolute brightness of a star.

multiverse In theoretical cosmology, a hypothetical set of universes of which our universe is just one of many.

neutrino A fundamental particle with very little mass and no electric charge created by radioactive decay and nuclear reactions.

nuclear fission A reaction in which a heavy nucleus such as uranium-235 splits into smaller fragments, releasing energy in the process.

nuclear fusion A reaction in which light atomic nuclei combine to form a heavier nucleus, releasing energy in the process.

nucleosynthesis The process in which new atomic nuclei are made from preexisting lighter atomic nuclei.

Planck era The period lasting from 0 to 10^{-43} seconds after the big bang during which the conditions were so extreme our laws of physics cannot describe them. All four fundamental forces were unified at this time.

quadrupole magnet A magnet with two sets of north and south poles, such as a configuration of four bar magnets arranged in an "X" with two north and two south poles in the center.

quantum mechanics The branch of physics that describes the motion and interaction of matter and light on the atomic and subatomic scale.

radial velocity The velocity of a galaxy or other object toward or away from an observer.

radio galaxy A type of galaxy that is very luminous at radio wavelengths.

recombination The process that occurred 240,000 to 300,000 years after the big bang in which particles including protons, neutron, and electrons paired up to form neutral atoms of hydrogen and helium.

redshift The shift of a galaxy or other object's emitted light toward redder (longer) wavelengths due to the expansion of the universe.

spectroscope A device used to analyze light spectra.

string theory The theory that the fundamental building blocks of the universe are tiny strands of energy that vibrate in eleven dimensions.

ultraviolet The portion of the electromagnetic spectrum with a wavelength just shorter than the blue end of the visible light spectrum but longer than the wavelength of the X-ray portion of the spectrum.

wave-particle duality The nature of light and matter to have characteristics of both particles (such as discrete amounts of energy) and waves (such as wavelength and frequency).

Further Information

Books

Hawking, Stephen. *A Brief History of Time*. New York: Bantam Books, 1998.

Rovelli, Carlo. *Seven Brief Lessons on Physics*. New York: Riverhead Books, 2014.

Websites

The 14-Billion Year History
https://www.cfa.harvard.edu/seuforum/
bb_popup_history3.htm
Watch a video simulation of the big bang and read about the universe in its first three minutes, first 300,000 years, and forward.

Webb Telescope & the Big Bang
http://jwst.nasa.gov/bigBangQandA.html
Read a short Q&A with Dr. John Mather, a Nobel Prize–winning physicist, about the big bang and how we study it.

Videos

Is Our Universe the Only Universe?
https://www.ted.com/talks/brian_greene_why_
is_our_universe_fine_tuned_for_life?
Explore theories of what may have come before the big
bang, including the multiverse, with theoretical physicist
Brian Greene.

Light Waves, Visible, and Invisible
http://ed.ted.com/lessons/light-waves-visible-
and-invisible-lucianne-walkowicz
Learn more about the electromagnetic light spectrum,
wavelengths, and frequency, as well as how our eyes
perceive light and how telescopes serve as virtual eyes.

Particle Fever
http://particlefever.com/
Watch an award-winning documentary about six scientists'
efforts to use the Large Hadron Collider to recreate the
conditions just after the big bang in order to find the
Higgs boson particle and validate the Standard Model
of cosmology.

Bibliography

Adams, W.S. "Obituary: Dr. Edwin P. Hubble." *The Observatory* 74 (1954): 32–35.

"Albert Einstein – Biographical." Nobelprize.org. 2014. Retrieved July 12, 2016. http://www.nobelprize.org/ nobel_prizes/physics/laureates/1921/einstein-bio.html.

"All About Neutrinos." *IceCube*. Retrieved July 12, 2016. https://icecube.wisc.edu/info/neutrinos.

"Arno Penzias – Biographical." Nobelprize.org. 2014. Retrieved July 12, 2016. http://www.nobelprize.org/ nobel_prizes/physics/laureates/1978/penzias-bio.html.

"Birth of the Universe." Retrieved July 12, 2016. http://abyss. uoregon.edu/~js/ast123/lectures/lec17.html.

Blair, Bill. "The Basics of Light." Johns Hopkins University. Retrieved July 19, 2016. http://www.pha.jhu.edu/~wpb/ spectroscopy/basics.html.

Bow, Erin. "Is the Universe a Bubble? Let's Check." Perimeter Institute for Theoretical Physics. July 17, 2014. https://www.perimeterinstitute.ca/news/universe- bubble-lets-check.

"CERN's Large Hadron Collider Recreates Big Bang Primordial Soup." *Tech Times*. February 11, 2016. http://www.techtimes.com/articles/132341/20160211/cerns-large-hadron-collider-recreates-big-bang-primordial-soup.htm.

"Discovering the Electromagnetic Spectrum." NASA. September 2013. http://imagine.gsfc.nasa.gov/science/toolbox/history_multiwavelength1.html.

"George Smoot – Biographical." Nobelprize.org. 2014. Retrieved July 12, 2016. https://www.nobelprize.org/nobel_prizes/physics/laureates/2006/smoot-bio.html.

Greene, Brian. *The Fabric of the Cosmos*. Documentary. July 25, 2012. Boston, MA: Nova.

Hawking, Stephen. "The Beginning of Time." *Stephen Hawking*. Retrieved July 12, 2016. http://www.hawking.org.uk/the-beginning-of-time.html.

"How an accelerator works." *CERN*. Retrieved July 12, 2016. http://home.cern/about/how-accelerator-works.

Hoyle, Fred. "Synthesis of the Elements in Stars." *Review of Modern Physics* 29, No. 4, October 1957: 547–650.

Isaacson, Walter. *Einstein: His Life and Universe*. New York: Simon and Schuster, 2007.

"Obtaining Astronomical Spectra – Spectrographs." *Australia Telescope National Facility*. Retrieved July 12, 2016. http://www.atnf.csiro.au/outreach/education/senior/astrophysics/spectrographs.html.

"Robert Woodrow Wilson – Biographical." Nobelprize.org. 2014. Retrieved July 12, 2016. http://www.nobelprize.org/ nobel_prizes/physics/laureates/1978/wilson-bio.html.

Rummler, Troy. "Looking for strings inside inflation." *Symmetry*. August 27, 2015. http://www. symmetrymagazine.org/article/august-2015/looking-for-strings-inside-inflation.

Singh, Simon. *Big Bang: The Origin of the Universe*. New York: HarperCollins Publishers Inc., 2004.

Soter, Steven, and Neil deGrasse Tyson. *Cosmic Horizons: Astronomy at the Cutting Edge*. New York: New Press, 2001.

Stephen Hawking's Universe: The Big Bang. Documentary. Edited by Scott McEwing. 1997. Arlington, VA: PBS.

Index

Page numbers in **boldface** are illustrations. Entries in **boldface** are glossary terms.

About the Author

Rachel Keranen is a writer based in Madison, Wisconsin. Her work focuses on science, software, and entrepreneurship. She's passionate about learning and loves taking deep dives into science and history. In addition to the books that she writes for Cavendish Square, such as *Evolution* and *The Composition of the Universe: The Evolution of Stars and Galaxies*, Keranen's previous work includes articles in the *Minneapolis/St. Paul Business Journal* and the *London Business Matters* magazine.

Keranen enjoys traveling, biking, and spending time near water. As a young girl, her parents often pulled her out of bed in the middle of the night to watch shooting stars and meteor showers.